"a knack for making the mundane, visual and interesting."

BOB PAMPLIN

"a wonderful story teller!"

JUSTIN FARRELL

" a very descriptive way with words!"

GWEN LEMBKE

"The pictures are adorable!"

HELENE JOHNSEN

"Too Funny!"

ADMIRAL MIKE MATHIS

"Thanks for the laugh!"

TOM & GERRI HIESTAND

"Very well written, made me laugh out loud."

DOUGLAS MORRISON

"Delightful."

SUZY BURDICK

"Always amusing"

KEITH ODERMAN

Life at
Two Ponds

Royalties benefit ELCA World Hunger

Kathy Hoffman

XULON PRESS

Xulon Press
2301 Lucien Way #415
Maitland, FL 32751
407.339.4217
www.xulonpress.com

Paperback ISBN-13: 978-1-66283-218-5
Ebook ISBN-13: 978-1-66283-219-2

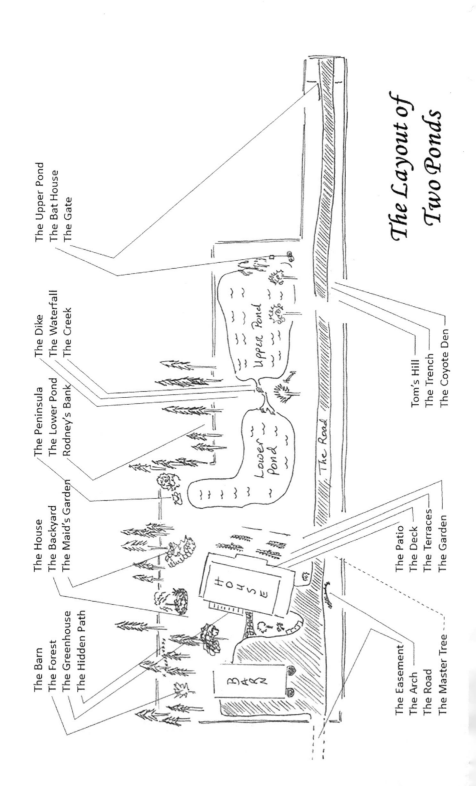

The Upper Pond
The Bat House
The Gate

The Dike
The Waterfall
The Creek

The Peninsula
The Lower Pond
Rodney's Bank

The House
The Backyard
The Maid's Garden

The Barn
The Forest
The Greenhouse
The Hidden Path

Tom's Hill
The Trench
The Coyote Den

The Patio
The Deck
The Terraces
The Garden

The Easement
The Arch
The Road
The Master Tree

Upper Pond

Lower Pond

The Road

HOUSE

BARN

The Layout of
Two Ponds

Other Books by the Author

"The Joyful Faces of Messiah"

Brooklyn Art Library, The Sketchbook Project, Volume 18

An illustrated collection of close-ups (eyes, nose, and mouth) of some of the 2021 members of Messiah Lutheran Church and Preschool in Vancouver, WA.

Dedication

To Brittany:

I was sorting through my pictures the other day and had the oddest little sensation. I smiled and thought, "I showed up!" And so did you, dear Brittany … and didn't we have fun! Donald, Mickey, and Holly Bear loved you … and so do I.

Brittany and Little Mickey

Acknowledgments

I am grateful for all the encouragement I've received from people who respond to my stories in person and on email. Suzy Sivyer and Justin Farrell, authors in their own right, have encouraged me to join their ranks. A special thanks to Helene Johnsen, Bob Pamplin, and Doug Morrison, who are usually the first to fire back happy responses to my stories.

Helene Johnsen has been a friend from grade school (and that's a long, long time ago). She has taken on the job of being my Muse. She read the book before it went to publishing. If you don't like it, I'll give you her contact information. But seriously, it helps to have a friendly cohort to keep me moving confidently toward the publishing deadlines.

Dorothy Stamp, my longtime neighbor, has laughed with me over coffee, almost every morning, for years. When she prods me for information, I start getting animated. Suddenly, I realize the stories might be fodder for a new book. (She really liked the Prom story … but you'll have to wait for it.)

I am grateful for my husband. Even though he's a man of few words (I have to use a tug-of-war approach to get feedback), he is definitely a rock in my life (that's a good thing … not like a pebble in my shoe). Because of his stability, I can look at life's situations and see the humor in them.

I love my best friend, Marg. Years ago, she told me I was "special." I didn't understand, but I remembered. Everyone should have a Marg in their life.

I am grateful for the people at Xulon Publishing for making it easy to concentrate on writing and illustrating and not have to worry about anything else.

I am grateful for the experience and insight provided by my brother, Kevin Walsh, regarding the importance of each step in the production and review process.

And finally, I'm grateful for Harry's Mom and her sisters, all long-gone. When they all got set up with email, they would chatter daily. I got to join their group. How fun was that! Each of us would report in by email about our days' events. If one of us took the day off, another would fire off an email with the subject line stating, "Where Are You?" Many of my stories included here were written for Mom, Alma and Diane. I remember them fondly.

Main Cast of Characters

Harry – My husband of 39 years. I hope you will come to know and love him as I do.

Carol – The wife of a man I worked with since 1970

Stephanie and Brittany – Carol's granddaughters

Janet – Carol's daughter

Jenae and Julie – Janet's daughters

Kiersten – Jenae's friend

Gary – Another man I worked with since 1970

Connie – Gary's wife

Michelle – Connie's daughter-in-law

Traci, Justine, Chelsea, Kimberly, Breanna – Connie's granddaughters

Emma – Connie's niece

Prologue

Overview

All my life I've been a competitive person. I frequently try to compete with Mother Nature, to bend the rules of physics, and most of all, to pit myself against my husband, our dogs, or little kids I don't even know. They never know we're in a competition … which is why they usually win! I keep trying to hide it, but sometimes, my competitive spirit runs amok … and when it does, the darndest things happen.

Organization

This autobiography has four parts. Join me now as I share the unlikely story of how Harry and I met and married and found our way to a hidden glen in the middle of a suburb of Vancouver, Washington, in Part One: "Journey to Two Ponds." Laugh with me as I goof up projects in and around the ponds in Part Two: "Living the Dream." Watch as overplanning fails and nimbleness becomes the name of the game in Part Three: "Tea Parties." Share in the sweet innocence of children related in anecdotes that took place away from Two Ponds in Part Four: "Stepping Out."

Punctuation

My editor must have been pulling her hair out because of my excessive use of ellipses (…). Ellipses are most often used to signify omitted text in quotations. However, one can also use an ellipsis to indicate a pause … or in my case, an afterthought or an aside. I grew into that style over the years. I hope you will enjoy the pace of this book a little more by pausing slightly … and often rolling your eyes … when you see an ellipsis.

Royalties

Give thanks for your blessings and be assured the royalties from your purchase will benefit the Evangelical Lutheran Church in America (ELCA) World Hunger. To make additional donations, visit www.elca.org.

"God richly provides for daily bread - the earth can produce enough food for everyone. Yet, many still go hungry. By providing immediate relief to those who are hungry, ELCA World Hunger meets basic needs and recognizes the universal human right to food. But ending hunger is about more than food. By connecting people with the resources they need to produce food and gain access to clean water, education, health care, and sources of income, long-term, sustainable change can be accomplished." -- ELCA World Hunger website

Life at
Two Ponds

PART ONE

JOURNEY TO TWO PONDS

Harry Meets Kate

July, 1982

Harry and I met in July, 1982. We were engaged in August and married in September that year. All in less than two months.

The key piece to our engagement story occurred in 1974. I was buying a house and was talking with Dad about insurance. He told me about a special policy he had, which would pay off the house in the event of his death. Well, that just sounded like free money even if I wouldn't be around to enjoy it. I went for it. I had a good State Farm agent, Lyle Cornelius. He had been an agent in Vancouver for ages. He tried to talk me out of getting that policy. He didn't feel good about selling it to a young, single woman. I was not to be deterred.

When Lyle died in 1981, his business was split between his son, Terry, and a new young agent fresh from Fruitland, Idaho. I got a letter from State Farm saying I was being reassigned to the new young agent, Harry Hoffman. Well, I was having nothing to do with that! I contacted State Farm and had my business switched over to Terry Cornelius. I was nothing, if not loyal!

I was very happy with Terry for a year, but then I made an unrelated business decision that caused me to look at all of my expenses with a keen eye. When I got a bill for the Mortgage Life policy, I finally realized Lyle had been right. I was still single after eight years, with no prospects in sight. That policy was not a good fit for my circumstances.

I had a real good idea of how insurance worked, and this is it: if you talk to your agent, your insurance rates go up. It's as simple as that. (As it turned out, I didn't know what I was talking about, but that has never hindered me.) There, at the bottom of the page, was the name of my insurance agent … it was the young agent who had come over from Fruitland, Idaho, a year earlier. I wondered why he was my agent for the life policy, but I didn't care. I was confident my insurance rates wouldn't go up, as long as I didn't talk to Terry!

I called Harry's office and asked to speak with him. They said he wasn't in the office in the afternoon and asked if I could call in the morning. I called several more times over the next two weeks, but since I was quite busy in the mornings, I was never able to connect with him. When we finally connected, I asked him about canceling the policy. He said I should just come in and sign the paperwork. I worked myself into a snit and asked him, "Won't it just cancel if I don't make the payment?"

"Well, yes … but that would be tacky."

Not wanting to be tacky, I made an appointment to go in and sign the paperwork.

The following Wednesday, I was feeling quite professional. I had on a white short-sleeve eyelet blouse and a slim knee-length fitted skirt … bright red. Anyone could see me coming!

I picked up my briefcase (not that I needed it, but it did make me look quite professional) and drove over to Harry's office in my bright green Volkswagen Bug. I dismounted (actually, at one inch shy of six feet, I unfolded myself from the Bug), grabbed my briefcase, threw my shoulders back, and marched into the office looking for that insurance agent. As it turned out, he was to my left, and the sun was to my right ... shining directly through the white eyelet blouse. I didn't have a clue, but Harry had seen all he needed to see to realize he wanted to get to know me better. Being a professional woman, we transacted our business, and he concluded by asking me if I had ever had an Estate Analysis done.

"No," I replied. "I don't believe I have."

"Well," he said, "let's make an appointment and we can do that."

"How much will it cost me?" I parried.

"Well, it won't cost you anything, but it will cost me $38," he countered.

It sounded to me like it was a pretty good deal. I was ready to go for it, but he said I would need to make an appointment for the next week. That was the last normal week of my life.

Estate Analysis

The next Wednesday, I showed up for the appointment. What a deal! I didn't even have to fill in any blanks. Harry read the questions from the form. I answered them. Some of the questions seemed a little personal. In fact, it seemed they didn't have a whole lot to do with an Estate Analysis. From time to time, I chose not to answer just for the heck of it. He took it in stride and moved on to the next question. I thought it was kind of strange I was getting away with not answering some of the questions. Come to think of it, a lot of those questions were fairly personal. But I was a professional woman, I dealt with them. Pretty soon the questions were over. I was a little disappointed … I was starting to enjoy it. He said it would take a couple of weeks to get the results and asked if I'd like to go out for a drink sometime. Not wanting to squirrel the deal, I had to string him along until I got the results of the Estate Analysis, so I agreed. We arranged to meet the following week.

We met after work and went to a quiet little bar with a backgammon table. He taught me how to play backgammon. I thought it was a slow game, like chess. At least that's the way I played it. I didn't realize it was supposed to go pretty fast. All the while, I was wondering if he'd ask me out for dinner. I knew how those things worked: One thing leads to another and before you know it, you're in a pickle … well, not me! We finished our drink. I was trying to come up with a good reason to decline a second. But no … one drink … that was it. Our date was over. I was still concerned about the Estate Analysis, so when he invited me to play racquetball as we were leaving, I accepted.

I showed up the next week for our racquetball game. I had never seen people play racquetball, but Marg (a close friend since 1975) and I had been trying to learn. It's a shame I hadn't seen it being played because I was playing like it was underhand tennis. Harry, on the other hand, knew how to play quite well. He never let on I wasn't doing it right. We played a couple of more times over the course of the next six weeks, always a fairly slow game, but getting faster each week. (After we were married, we tried to play one more time. Harry played like it was supposed to be played. I took a direct shot to the right cheek … and I'm not talking about where I smile. The bruise lasted for a couple of weeks. The bruise to my ego lasted longer! No more racquetball for me!)

Every time he invited me out, I accepted. I didn't want anything to get in the way of the Estate Analysis. Our dates never included dinner, and I started losing a little bit of weight here and there. But we did talk a lot … about everything. At one point Harry mentioned something about a list. He fired off six things on his list for a life partner. As he stated them, one by one, I found myself thinking, "Well, I qualify for that … Well, I qualify for that … Well, I qualify for that."

Then he turned to me and said, "Do you have a list?"

Of course, I had no such thing … but I was not to be outdone. I am competitive, you know, so I fired off a list of six qualities

I would be looking for in a man. One of them was persistence ... another patience ... and four more. And there it was ... my list was out there. It probably would have been a good idea to remember the list but I wasn't that smart. At any rate, Harry was patient and persistent. He was also much less risk-averse than I was ... and I knew it.

I'm in Love!

We spent Sunday, August 8, on the Lewis River with lots more talking. Toward the end of the day, I had a moment of clarity … I saw deep within his soul and realized there was a lot of depth to this man I had drastically overlooked. We made a date to meet for pizza on Tuesday, two days hence.

On Monday morning, as I was backing out of my driveway, I heard a hissing noise. The tire of my Volkswagen was resting kind of funny on the curb, and air was escaping from the tire. I moved the car quickly so I would have enough air to limp to the gas station and get it refilled. My fifty-year-old neighbor was backing out of his driveway and saw me standing there looking at the tire.

"Is everything okay?" he asked.

With that, I burst into tears! "No," I sobbed.

"What's the matter?" he asked.

I was able to pause long enough to blurt out, "I'm in love!"

And there it was! I hadn't realized it until that point. Tears were pouring down my face. I don't know exactly what my neighbor was thinking, but he got out of there fast. I was a mess for the next day and a half. I had forgotten all about the Estate Analysis.

When Harry came over on Tuesday, we sat at the dining room table, no pizza in sight. We had a list of life issues to discuss. We got right to it. We discussed every issue, compromising, when necessary, but never compromising principles. Eventually, we finished the list. The time had come. (About a week earlier the subject of marriage had come up. Not wanting to push me too fast, Harry said if we were to be married, I would have to be the one to propose.) The time had come … I knew it … he knew it. There was a major lull in our conversation. I had known him for less than four weeks! I didn't have the courage to take the first step. Harry took charge and asked me to marry him. I took the biggest chance of my lifetime and said yes. I've never regretted it!

Getting to Know You

We spent the following month meeting my family, individually and collectively. Everyone was chatty getting to know this man ... I learned a lot about him, but I had no idea Harry was a man of few words. Over time, I learned when you get married it starts a lifetime of discovery. I'm afraid I discovered Harry truly was a man of few words when I would whisper sweet nothings in his ear:

"I love you, Harry."

"Ditto."

We were engaged. Harry got a kit from the car store and we installed cruise control on his little Scirocco. Piece of cake. We worked well together! A good team.

It had been a hectic month. Being a truly good team player, Harry left all the wedding planning to me and said he'd just show up. The night before we got married, I insisted we go out to dinner and not talk about the wedding at all. It was nice. At the end of the evening, I was a little bemused. "Say," I asked hesitantly, "did you ever get the results of that Estate Analysis?"

"Oh, that?" he commented, offhandedly, "I never sent it in ... you weren't worth that much."

A part of me felt betrayed. I didn't know whether to be insulted or to laugh. I chose to laugh.

Harry and Kate Get Married

He moved into my house and made it his own. (I sneezed for two weeks, fearing I was allergic to my new husband. But it turned out I was just allergic to the dust that showed up as we were melding our households.) We lived happily there for four years.

A few months after the wedding, Harry got another kit for cruise control, this time for the Suburban. For some reason, the installation didn't go as smoothly as when we were engaged.

We worked very hard on a project and then just stopped for a while until we found another project. The first project was putting in two decks. A large deck off the back and a medium deck on the far side of the backyard. After the decks were finished, we got a small rototiller. Harry tilled up most of the remaining backyard, about 30' by 50'. We went to a garden nursery in Albany, Oregon, and got massive quantities of seeds. We selected several varieties of each type of plant. We just wanted to try out every variation … all in one year! After we got the garden planted, we stopped. Every night we would come home, have a little glass of wine, and appreciate sitting on the deck and watching the garden grow. We talked about the future. We created a five-year plan: (i) we would purchase five acres of land, (ii) we would purchase a large rototiller to till our five acres. Harry said we would not get the large rototiller until we got the property. I agreed. It was a good plan. Our plan went awry.

The next year, unbeknownst to me, we purchased a huge Troy-Bilt rototiller. It was ever so much easier to till the whole backyard up with a huge Troy-Bilt rototiller! After the backyard was tilled up, Harry still had the tiller gene fidgeting with his brain. He was looking covetously at the front yard until I put my foot down hard. Perhaps that's why he got wanderlust.

Wanderlust

Being a State Farm agent, meant Harry was looking at houses … really nice houses … every day … taking pictures and measuring. After four years, he was getting more and more anxious to upgrade from our little 1200-square-foot ranch-style home. In fact, four years was the longest he had lived anywhere.

In the spring of 1986, Harry said he'd like to take me to see a house nearby. We drove down a long tree-lined lane toward Blueberry Hill, passing four ponds (the last two of which had been drained) until finally the view opened up across a gully, to a little two-story daylight basement house at the top of a hill, overlooking the ponds. I fell in love with the possibilities. Within two months it was ours. One of the four ponds belonged to the next-door neighbors. As part of the transaction, they purchased a second pond and we purchased the remaining two ponds and the house. We moved in on the 15th of June. Harry sneezed non-stop for a month until the trees stopped their procreation activities.

Little House on the Hill

What's in a Name

One day, Harry and I were driving along to some function or another. I decided it was time to name our property. I posed the question to Harry and invited him to come up with something. Just for fun, I threw out names to describe our property: "Fern Gully" … "Willow Bank" … "Gully View." A lot of names came to mind, perhaps because I've heard them before. Some were just lame: "Maple Lane" … "Blueberry Gully." I did have some pride. More than anything I wanted our place to be named "Chicken Creek Kennels." To me, that name is steeped in romance, but Chicken Creek was the next creek over, and we didn't need the word Kennels because we had stopped breeding West Highland White Terriers by that time.

I couldn't get Harry interested in the topic. Finally, in desperation, I threw out "Two Ponds," but only as a segue to "Pon Deux," which was where I really wanted to end up. I could see our return address … "Hoffman at Pon Deux." It felt good … and made me a little hungry. My man of few words said, "Two Ponds." What followed was a wimpy attempt to get him to appreciate my fractured French version, but with those two words, he had spoken. It was a done deal. We lived at "Two Ponds." Conversation over!

Two Ponds consists of 1.85 acres stretching north and south over the landscape. The house on the hill has a commanding view of the ponds. With all the trees surrounding our property, it's hard to see any of the neighboring homes. Consequently, if we didn't like our view, we just changed it ... and we did so, many times, over the years. But first I named everything so Harry and I could communicate.

"The Barn" ... aka the Workshop

"The House"

"The Asphalt" ... The parking area between the Barn and the House.

"The Greenhouse" ... because who can remember to say Sunporch.

"The Forest"

"The Backyard"

"The Maid's Garden" ... In the early years, as we were looking forward to retirement, Harry started talking about having a live-in maid to cook and clean. Well, you know that didn't happen, but when we remodeled the house in the mid-90s, we framed the window so it could be easily changed to a door. In our dreams, the Maid would have a two-room suite at the far-end of the top floor, including a bathroom ... there would be a bridge across the grass pathway on the east side of the house, to an ivy-covered sitting area. Our friends, Ted and Cheryl, gave us some leftover azaleas which became a fixture in The Maid's Garden.

"The Deck" ... on the main level

"The Patio" ... on the lower level

"The Terraces" … five cascading eight-foot-wide strips of lawn featuring espaliered apple trees. The Terraces stair-step down to the ponds.

"The Arch" … an eight-foot metal trellis that fought with a maple tree and lost. Because it is dressed with Virginia Creeper, it's hard to tell it is anything but a perfect arch.

"The Road" … a driveway road running the full length of the property. It occasionally washes out, leaving a deep, impassable hole. We're very happy to have an alternate egress to the north.

"The Easement" … the egress to the north.

"The Lower Pond" … unceremoniously named for its position in the landscape

"The Upper Pond" … same reason

"The Peninsula" … an earthen outcrop separating our property from the property of the neighbors to the east.

"The Dike" … an earthen dam separating the two ponds

"The Creek" … the upper portion of a creek that cuts through The Dike.

"The Waterfall" … the water pouring from The Creek to a lower level. The water splits into two unnamed trickles before dropping into The Lower Pond.

"Tom's Hill" … the area west of our road.

"The Trench" … the drainage trench at the base of Tom's Hill.

"The Bat House" … Harry built a bat house using a full four-by-eight sheet of plywood. It was a bottom-less salt-box with about six parallel walls. He built it … but would they come? Maurice, our neighbor, helped Harry get it up on the flagpole. Every time Harry wandered down the road, he'd approach the pole, bend from the waist, and examine the ivy. It was humorous to see Maurice do the same thing: approach the pole, bend from the waist, examine the ivy. Dorothy and I thought they were funny. They must have had Japanese ancestry. Then, a full year later, Harry came back to our house all excited. He had seen bat guano! We had bats. I went down the road, approached the pole, bent from the waist, and sure enough, there was a little bat guano on the ivy leaves. I called Dorothy over. She approached the pole, bent from the waist, and examined the ivy. Japanese ancestry must be contagious.

"The Gate" … The southern-most portion of our long narrow acreage, near the mailbox (unnamed).

"Rodney's Bank" … the eastern side of both ponds.

"The Berm" … a mistake which was eventually leveled but kept its name.

"The Coyote Den" … a hollowed-out area beneath a clump of maples. It looks like it could house a passel of critters, but doesn't.

"The Master Tree" … a major fir tree at the bottom of our hill that is no more. The Master Tree cast way too much shadow on our house and eventually met its demise on a quiet summer day. The tree guys laid that baby right along our property line. It was a thing of beauty to see it come down with precision. About five or ten minutes later a man from two blocks away drove up our driveway to see what was happening. He had been in his rest room … resting. When the Master Tree dropped, he got splashed!

"The Garden" … the location varies year to year.

We didn't name everything all at once, but whenever we needed to talk about an area, it got a name.

PART TWO

LIVING THE DREAM

Staking out Territory

There was a whole lot of work to be done. Harry took the first step and filled the ponds. And then he sat down on the porch. We spent every day going to work in the daytime and sitting on the porch in the evening. "What in the world?" I wondered in dismay. There was a whole lot of work to be done ... way more work than one person could handle. We were supposed to be a team! As we sat there, Edvard Munch's painting "Scream" played repeatedly in my head. I vowed I would not get up until we both got up together ... we had to be a team! I waited ... silently! I was determined to wait as long as it took, even if the weeds ate our house!

Waiting for "Our Team" to Get Going

And then months later, Harry stood up, got the huge Troy-Bilt rototiller and the chipper-shredder out of the garage, wheeled them across the dike, and proceeded to rape and pillage the hillside. With the shreddings, he built a path around that section of the pond. It lasted for 35 years … and counting. When he finished, he sat back down in his rocking chair. I didn't understand, but I could see that our team was up and running.

The best place for a garden was on the north end of the property. I was always amending the soil, having become adept at using the huge Troy-Bilt rototiller. One day, my neighbor Brad, a great big teddy bear of a man, peeked over the arborvitae hedge and commented as I was working in the garden … digging, tilling, hoeing, raking, spreading. "That garden is the bane of your existence!" Not having a real clear idea at the time what bane meant, I just scratched my head, smiled, and agreed. After all, I did spend a lot of hours fussing with that soil.

That fall, I wondered if I could start willow from a switch. I stuck about a dozen skinny little branches in the soil. The next year, I check to see if they had rooted. The roots extended for eight feet in opposite directions! That didn't seem to be a real good idea for the future! Up came the willow trees, and in went a lot of seeds. I had visions of an abundance of flowers. I've had that same vision of abundance of flowers so many times in my years at Two Ponds. However, this time it actually worked. When the flowers started to get to nursery height, I invited people to bring their pots over and pot up some flowers from my treasure trove. 1996 was a grand and glorious year!

In 1997, Harry got his hands on a bulldozer. Away went my garden to be used as fill in the Forest, thirty yards away. Harry's brother Jon was called into service with his contracting skills. Up went a great big workshop. It was gigantic! I had no say in the matter (well maybe I did, but it was pretty exciting all the same), except for the size of the parking area between the workshop and the house. Harry was lobbying for two-parts gravel, one-part front yard. I was lobbying for two-parts front yard, one-part gravel. Somehow, we managed to split the difference and be happy about it.

Harry painted the workshop red. I named it … "The Barn."

Muck-Muddy

March 2014

L ate March was chilly and wet. Harry suggested I pull the plug on the Lower Pond because a lot of rain was in the forecast. A good rainstorm would help our pond to self-dredge. The Lower Pond is L-shaped and about 100' long by 30 to 50' wide. Draining the pond is a very simple process. All you have to do is attach the cable to the trailer hitch on the car and gently pull the large flat banjo-shaped steel contraption from the mouth of the twelve-inch outlet in the bottom of the pond. Since it slips out sideways, it's pretty simple to remove, but when the pond is full, you can't do it by hand … too much water pressure.

The dogs always love to go for a ride, no matter how far we go. I piled the three dogs in the car, drove fifty yards down to the Lower Pond, hitched the cable to the car, got back in, rolled down the window, and proceeded to edge forward … Nothing. I removed the brake, said a little prayer, "Oh Lord, Please Don't Make This Harder Than It Needs To Be!" and turned to watch my impending triumph. I edged forward … ZING! … the cable snapped in a weak spot. I backed up and took a look at the damage. I guess cables don't last forever. I climbed down to water's edge, grabbed what was left of the cable, attached a heavy-duty string from an old, abandoned dog leash to the cable, got back in the car, took off the brake, said my little prayer again while edging forward, and … ZING! … it snapped again.

I got out and took a look. This was obviously not going to be a simple procedure. The water level was only down a few feet, so I thought maybe I could put the sixteen-foot aluminum boat in and horse the plug up by hand. I hefted the boat around and slowly shoved it over the rocks, being careful not to puncture the shell. It's a pretty good boat … very serviceable. The oar was about fifty yards further up the road on the bank of the Upper Pond. Too far. I was pretty sure I could make do with a small three-foot branch. It worked fine. I "paddled" over to the outlet, got the cable, pulled it up, and slick as a whistle I unplugged the pond. A little eddy began. Success! Not much harder than it needed to be.

Harry had mentioned it took about ninety minutes to empty the pond so, since I had a little time and since the water level was down a bit, I thought I'd meander around in the boat and pull out some of the three-and four-inch-diameter branches. They looked unsightly when the water level was down. (Were you paying attention? … I wasn't.) I pulled up this one, that one and the other one. By the time I had four six-foot limbs in the boat, I looked around to where I had planned to off-load them. "Gee," I thought, "the water level is getting a little low." I'd have to muck my way through about ten feet of wet mud to get to a safe spot. I thought I might as well go to the other end of the pond since it might be easier to off-load the branches. I heard a loud sucking noise and instantly knew I had very little time left. I pushed and paddled my way to the bend in the pond, getting momentarily stuck. As I navigated the shallow water and edged my boat toward the far end, I realized there was a large branch in the way. Since I was already having trouble maneuvering the boat, I decided I'd better retreat. Too late! The boat was stuck in the worst possible spot. There was still a little time. There were only three inches of water left to drain. I stood up, bent over, grabbed the sides of the boat, and lunged my body forward … the boat moved an inch. I lunged again … another inch. Lunge, Lunge, Lunge … inch, inch, inch. Lunge like crazy … freedom! I took my trusty stick and in grand Venetian style, backed the boat right up to the outlet. Done. There was nowhere else to go, and the pond had been emptied. Evidently it only takes about 30 to 45 minutes to empty a partially emptied pond!

Off-loading the boat was the next order of business. Getting the limbs any distance closer to the shore would help. I lifted one huge limb and hefted it to the shore eight feet away. It only flew three feet, but it was the right direction. The next one was better. I hefted it like a pole-vaulter would. After heaving two more limbs and the rusted "banjo" plug, the boat was empty but for me and my trusty stick. I pushed the stick down into the fresh mud calculating I'd likely sink six to eight inches with every step. My shoes were only three inches high. Once you know the inevitable, it's easy to take the first step. And so, I took it. I felt the cold wet mud on my socks and felt the mud and water seeping into my shoes. No time to dilly-dally. Step, step, step … splat … crawl to freedom!

It really wasn't that bad.

I went around to where the limbs were waiting and pulled all but the first of them out of the pond. The first one would have to remain in the pond for another day. The dogs were still waiting

in the car thirty feet up the road. I knew I had to get the boat out
of the pond because we were expecting rain and the boat is not
intended to be a submersible! I got some cable and light rope
and shook my head as I looked at the boat: the stern was facing
me, butted up against the outlet pipe. Oh, well! I sidled down
the bank taking my first step sideways into the mud with my
right foot, knowing it was going to be slippery. I thought just
maybe, if I slid my right foot a little, I could find my footing.
It seemed like a good plan. Oops … I was sliding a lot more
than a little. It was going to get ugly if I ended up doing the
sideways splits, so I abandoned the bank and stepped in with
my left foot, too … Whoop-whoop-whoop! Both feet slipped
out from under me as I plopped on my rear. Knowing there
was no hope of staying clean, I just let the ten-year-old inside
me slide on my seat, down the slick bank to the boat. It was
short, but it was fun. I trudged around to the other side of the
boat, and while I was hooking up the handle, I sunk deeper
and deeper into the wet mud … twelve inches. I had to pull
against the suction to wiggle my shod foot out. I really didn't
want to abandon my shoes! I lifted my right leg into the boat
and tried to do the same with my left leg, but by that time, my
left leg was about fifteen inches into the mud. I tried and tried
and tried again … No can do! Finally, I got a brilliant idea: if I
put my right foot back in the mud, I could pull my left one out
… Wrong. I got my left one out and helped it into the boat but
couldn't get enough leverage to get the right one out … by that
time, the right one was fifteen inches into the mud. At least my
legs weren't cramping … yet. Then I got the ultra-brilliant idea
to do something with both feet. Success of sorts! I discovered
I could get myself deeper into the mud by fooling around with
both feet … I was going in the wrong direction up to my knees!

Up to My Knees in Muck!

It was time to review my options: (1) I wondered if I should call for help. But no one was around at noon on a Monday. (2) I wondered if I should wait for Harry to come home. It was kind of cold, and that didn't seem a likely alternative. Besides, my pride wouldn't let me entertain that option very long. (3) I thought I might dig myself out by hand (my trusty stick was long gone). As I started digging, I gave myself a pep talk about there always being at least three ways of doing anything. SHLOOP (I dug with my gloved hands) … SPLOT (I tossed the mud aside). SHLOOP … SPLOT … SHLOOP … SPLOT, and so on. After about eight handfuls, I was down to about six inches. Both feet came out, and I clambered into the boat for a little rest and reconnoitering. (In retrospect, it would have been better to climb in the boat to hook up the pulling gear, rather than hook it while I was slowly sinking.) I got out of the boat. With the rope and cable in hand, I looked very much like a poster girl for evolution: I crawled out of the primordial ooze and up the bank on all fours.

Once up, I removed as much muck as possible from my shoes, pant legs, and seat. Then I began the laborious process of pulling the boat out of the mud … backwards. Heave … heave … heave. The last heave almost toppled me over. The boat was out of the pond, on the grass and turned over in moments. I picked up the spare rope and cable, put it under the boat, and then trudged over to the car where the dogs were waiting patiently. There was no way I was going to get in the car all muck-muddy, so I stripped down to my undies and tee shirt, put the offensive clothes in the trunk, and got in the car. It's really nice there are no neighbors close by! I was actually pretty clean without my mucky coverings. I drove up to the barn, put the little dogs in the pen, drove down to the garage, unloaded the dirty clothes into a pile, closed up everything, and hit the shower!

The next day, I rinsed the clothes in the mop bucket watching chunks of mud fall from the seat of my britches, gloves, sleeves, and pant legs. It fast became a funny memory. Replacement cable … lots of it … went on my shopping list!

Go Left or Go Right

One year, there was a severe heat warning for the whole weekend. For weeks, I had been anticipating getting out in the boat to do some pond maintenance in the Upper Pond. It looked like the perfect day to do so.

I did, however, have a couple of things that worried me: first, I don't like the idea of getting my feet wet, so I put on my water boots; and second, I don't like the idea of getting my gloves wet, especially when there's a hole in one of the fingers. I worried about those two things for a little while and then decided to just get out and get to work. I knew I'd probably get a little wet … I always do.

Once in the boat, it was easy to get around. I pulled quite a bit of floating pond-plant stuff into the boat. (They looked like four leaf clovers about the size of a silver dollar on a six-inch stem.) It was easy to get the plants in the boat because they weren't rooted in the silt. I pulled and pulled on a particularly thick stand of plants. They were all connected … more and more and more pond-plants came into the boat by the armload. (My hands were wet, but my feet were still dry.) Soon the middle of the boat filled up with pond-plant debris, and the pile started growing my way. Water trickled toward me and soaked my britches as I was sitting on the bench seat. But I was in the middle of a massive collection effort and wasn't about to stop. I pulled in another couple of bushels. Since they were all matted together, I just about had it in my lap before I was able to stop and empty the boat.

Having filled the boat beyond what I could manage, I rowed over to the bank and tried to throw it from the boat to the bank. As I threw an arm-load from the boat to the bank, the boat moved a couple of feet away from the bank. It's simple physics … "For every action, there is an equal and opposite reaction." My armload of debris ended up in the water. Oh, well! A smaller armload of debris made it to the bank. I had the beginnings of a system: empty the boat, bail the excess water, go back for more.

I filled the boat a second time.

Having already had some success emptying the boat, I decided to try something new. Now, you know, I'm not stuu-pid! I've taken physics, engineering, and math. I know how things work, especially on water. I couldn't quite get the boat next to the stationary log on the bank because there were underwater branches in the way. I stood in the boat and managed to sling one leg on top of the log. (I was still a little worried about getting water in my boots even though my socks and my britches were drenched. My toes were the last holdout … I continued to worry about getting them wet.)

As I was standing in the boat, half-propped on land and half-propped in the boat, I noticed the boat was slowly drifting away from the bank. I didn't realize it at the time, but this was one of those times in life when there were only two choices: go left or go right.

Have you heard of Jean-Claude Van Damme? He's famous for doing the splits. He's been in over fifty movies and has performed over 80,000 splits. Once in a movie, I saw him do the splits and then raise himself back up through sheer thigh muscle control. How hard could it be?

And so … although it looked like I only had two choices – go left or go right – I chose to pull a move like Jean-Claude Van Damme did. In that split second, I believed I could salvage the situation by pulling my feet together thus bringing the boat to the shore. I was wrong! I had passed the point of no return. In one of those rare moments where time stands still, I realized the laws of physics were going to rule the situation. As for my worries about getting my feet wet … in that split second all my worries were gone.

Jean-Claude Van "Dame"

There's a Bible verse in 1 Thessalonians that says "In everything give thanks." I gave thanks I still had my glasses on and my head didn't go under the water. I was aware enough of what was going on to appreciate the bubbles rising from my boots. This was one of those times when it's good to have a lot of vegetation around the pond to hide the obvious from the neighbors (or one's husband) should they happen to be watching. As I was flailing to right myself, I was grateful the water didn't seem all that cold. I got back to work covered in duckweed from neck to toe, water streaming from the pockets of my jacket, and enjoyed the fact I had nothing left to worry about!

And Then Some

Harry and I both knew we were allergic to dog dander. Nevertheless, from the get-go we decided we wanted dogs. And, more than having them, we wanted to breed them. We raised four litters of West Highland White Terriers, thoroughly enjoying all the challenges. One time, with two litters born a month apart, we had thirteen Westies. Thank goodness the preponderance were puppies. After the Westies, we usually had three dogs at once. Over the years, I've fought repeatedly, trying to claim my rightful place as second in the pack … and lost.

We got two little Corgi puppies in 2016 … litter mates. Lucy was a little sausage. Holding Angie, on the other hand, was like holding an armful of Jell-O. They both ate well and did the resulting activity well, too. They played like crazy for about one and one-half hours each morning, and then they just seemed to sleep the rest of the day. Each time I walked by and saw them lift their heads, I had to run them out to the grass for a little break. They would wrestle nearby for a few minutes, then we would come back in, and they would go back to sleep and grow some more.

When they were small, I could easily manage them as one armful. I would take them out of their individual crates, unlock and open two doors, and carry them outside gracefully … while still not waking Harry … or dropping them. Before long, they had grown so much I could no longer manage them together. Angie didn't seem to care if she made it to the grass or not, so I carried her and let Lucy pad along behind me, with no detours!

Lucy was initially a little better about coming when I called her. We used her like a bungie cord to get Angie to come, too. "Lucy ... COME!" usually brought both of them on the run. In the years to come, I discovered it was more about the possibility of missing out on getting a treat that brought Angie on the run.

One day, the Girls had been sleeping for a while, and I was ready to go to work at 2:00 p.m.-ish. I let them out for a last break. Lucy got right to business and did what had to be done. So did Angie. "Lucy ... COME!" Lucy came, but Angie didn't. I got Lucy in the house and then tackled my problem child. "Angie ... COME!" She just sat there looking at me. "Angie ... COME!" No response. Finally, she stood up, took one step toward me, and collapsed face-first on the lawn. I laughed, gently picked her up and took her into the house. She was still asleep ... with her eyes open!

Fred

We had a little visitor under the sink, but some mouse bait took care of that problem in just one day. No more problems under the sink. All our problems were resolved … or were they?

One night, I was heading upstairs when I heard Harry say, "Ohhhh!" in a very strange but gentle way. "We have a mouse." He had just seen a cute little mouse scurry across the floor and under the credenza. Maybe it hadn't been such a good idea to put wheels under the credenza, after all. Harry took Jack, (Border Collie) and Angie and Lucy (Corgi puppies) outside while I went in search of a dowel rod, a curtain rod, or a yard stick. I found an expandable ceiling duster. When I came back, I saw "Fred" stealthily creeping toward the water dish. He stopped at the side of the dish but evidently didn't see me watching him. I thought it might be a good idea to open the door and guide him outside …How hard could it be? I opened the door, and Angie raced in. I got her out and warned Harry about my plan. I carefully looked back at the water dish. Surprisingly, Fred was still sitting there. With that, Cocoa Bean (Chihuahua) ran out of the house, passing me in a blur. I looked back at the water dish … Fred was gone. I dusted under the credenza, finding toys that had been missing for months … but no Fred.

We bagged it for the evening. I went upstairs to the computer to check my email. Harry put all four dogs to bed and retired to read. After a bit, Harry heard someone lapping up water and wondered, "Hey, didn't I put all the dogs in their crates?" He looked over at the water dish to find Fred sitting there on the edge having a little refreshment. Harry had a plan that involved a wastebasket, but Fred was too fast and found refuge under our massive sofa recliner. (One point for FRED.)

The next day, I was playing with Angie and Lucy on the lawn when they suddenly decided to book it for the patio. I trailed at a slower pace. As I approached, I saw Angie chewing on something. As I got a little closer, I wondered if it was a pinecone. She spit it out just long enough for me to see it wasn't a pinecone. With my face scrunched up in disgust, I grabbed her up by the scruff of the neck hollering, "Spit it out, spit it out!" It never came out, and it wasn't in her mouth. I know, because I stuck my finger in there and dug around for anything not connected to her jaw. I bent over and examined the cushion she had been sitting on and was horrified to find a leg bone and other skeletal pieces. Was it FRED? Ick. I hoped my face wouldn't freeze with that expression. At the very same time, Harry was at the office using Amazon Prime to find humane mouse traps. Was it too little, too late?

That night we were sitting quietly, watching TV, when Harry said, "Fred's under the curtains."

I craned my neck and replied, "Where? … I can't see him."

And Harry, in typical Harry-fashion, said, "That's the point."

As I recovered from the slur, I commented, "Maybe we should encourage him to go outside."

Harry got up to open the door, and I saw Fred scurry back under the credenza. I swear he looked just like a little wind-up toy. I was pleased to see him, sort of. Angie saw him too and took up a post in front of the credenza waiting for him to come out to play.

Angie Waits for Fred

The following day, Harry came home with three different kinds of humane mouse traps. He said he had been about to order one when he saw a comment announcing, "Customers like you are also interested in these products." Below that were two more types of traps. Then he saw a button labelled, "Order All Three Now," so he poked it. Two days later, we had three humane mouse traps. The big one is a little larger than a one-pound box of chocolates. (I didn't mind making that comparison because

I had stopped eating candy.) The other two (one of which was a corner trap) had see-through tops.

We had a great time that evening. Harry was sitting there reading before I came home and thought he heard something. He looked into the corner trap back next to the credenza, under the four-foot-high shelf (watch your head … oops), but there was nothing. He looked at the big trap, but since he couldn't see inside, he shook it … nothing. He sat back down. That happened a few more times during the evening. He bonked his head twice more in the process; I didn't check as often, so I only bonked my head once. Each time we checked, we rocked the trap back and forth, but there was no mouse. Too bad this trap didn't have a see-through top. Finally, we went to bed to read before retiring. Angie bumps around in her metal crate from time to time making a little noise, so when we heard TINK, TINK, TINK, Harry said, "Angie … Quiet!" When she didn't settle down, we thought it might have been one of the traps. Harry turned on the light and went over to check. Shake, shake, shake … Nothing … not even a head-bonk this time. We finished reading a little while later, shut off the light, and retired.

TINK, TINK, TINK.

"Angie … Quiet!"

TINK, TINK, TINK.

"Jack … go to bed!"

TINK, TINK, TINK.

"Kate … go see if you can hear where that's coming from!"

I got halfway across the room and said I was pretty sure it was coming from the large trap.

For reasons I'm too embarrassed to mention, I decided to go back to bed at that point. Harry put on his robe, took the trap out through the garage, shut the garage door, and opened the trap on the lawn. A little dazed from his roller-coaster evening, Fred jumped out and scurried for the safety of the grass around the pond. We think he actually entered the trap about 4:00 o'clock in the afternoon ... when Harry got his first inkling.

We went back to bed, thankful Fred was back in HIS element, not OURS. Angie bumped around in her metal crate a little ... TWANG, TWANG, TWANG. Jack was quietly watching the whole scene play out from the comfort of his crate ... he rarely stirred after going to bed. We went to bed happily knowing the difference between TINK and TWANG ... and comforted by the fact we'll never know if Fred was pregnant.

I think we earned a point, but I think Fred deserved one, too. Too bad I wasn't keeping score!

Getting Set for Mothers' Day

On the Saturday before Mothers' Day, I ...

- got out of bed at 5:30 a.m.,
- took care of the bird and dogs,
- went back to sleep on the couch,
- got up two hours later,
- prayed,
- wondered how many people would RSVP,
- waited for Harry to come home with the dogs, and
- prepared for Sunday School.

As I was just about finished, Harry came in and poured himself a bowl of cereal. Apparently, he'd been home for an hour, and I didn't realize it. Oops!

Harry left for the club to do his exercise routine, while I ...

- got on the treadmill,
- pulled out the vacuum,
- started the laundry,
- made Split Pea soup for the Mothers' Day dinner,
- moved the furniture,
- vacuumed,

- cleaned the bird cage,

- mopped,

- changed the laundry,

- potted some spider plants, and

- planted some sweet peas in front of the patio.

Harry came home. It was time for a break, so I …

- made and served lunch,

- drank chocolate coffee on the patio with Harry,

- talked about life and plants,

- scooped poop so Harry could mow,

- potted more plants including geraniums,

- snipped some old tulips,

- picked some amazing dandelions in their prime,

- cleaned up my mess,

- straightened up the garage,

- finished the laundry,

- spiced up the Split Pea soup,

- chopped a nice salad for an appetizer,

- put the dinner in the oven,

- ate salad with Harry while watching TV,

- took a quick shower,

- made cookies for dessert,

- ate dinner,

- baked brownies for the Mothers' Day party,
- cooked brown rice, also for the party,
- ate cookies with Harry,
- cleaned up the kitchen,
- prepared three kinds of juices for the party,
- put the rice in a chafing dish, and
- checked the computer for RSVPs: no update.

Finally, there was just enough time for me to …

- run the dishwasher,
- put out my vitamins for the next four weeks,
- put some finishing touches on the dessert, and
- hit the hay at 11:10 p.m.

On Sunday, I …

- got out of bed at 6:00 a.m.,
- took care of the bird and dogs,
- had a cup of coffee,
- prayed,
- dozed a little,
- started moving in earnest at 8:30 a.m.,
- saw Harry off for his golf game
- set up the table for dinner,
- had breakfast,
- got dressed,

- cut some rhodies and andromeda for church,

- poured a traveling mug of chocolate coffee, and

- set out for church.

When I got to church, I ...

- visited with the regulars,

- set up the Sunday School room,

- went back to the sanctuary for worship.

After worship, Cousin Cathy and I went to the classroom before the kids came running in. We were studying Romans that week. I had pulled 41 verses from Romans that had great life lessons. For the past few weeks, we had been all about understanding Paul.

I had a game ready. I gave the kids the paraphrased verses and told them they had to figure out which paraphrased version went with the actual Bible verse I would read to them.

I started with some easy ones. They were participating, but I could tell their attention was starting to wander, so I congratulated the next person to make a match and told the other seven kids, "Elena has three correct answers now, and when she gets to five, she'll be eligible to leave." All they had to do before they left for the day was get five correct matches. BOOM! Everyone's mind was in the game.

The verses got harder, but the kids were listening and responding. Even the one little guy who likes to hang back was trying to get a match. The other thing they had to do before leaving class was turn in a quiz question (and answer) for the final exam. Timmy and Anna started working on their quiz questions before we finished the matching part. I told them that was fine, but they'd have to make up another quiz question with everyone else after we finished the matching game. BOOM! ... back in the game, again!

On and on we went. Finally, the man in charge came and said the adults had been dismissed. The kids had gotten thirty matches! I told them they didn't have to do a quiz question, but they did have to bring me one match they'd made and tell me why they liked it.

The one who is normally reticent came up first. I accepted his match and his reason (thankful he was participating). The others came one by one and successfully gave me very good reasons. One little boy was frantic. He had two verses with their paraphrased matches. Both were long. Lots of words. He couldn't remember which one went with which. I told him he had to figure it out. He still couldn't cut through all the wordiness (neither could I). After all the other students had given me their reasoning and had left, my little guy was still struggling. I told him he could give me just the paraphrased version but he had to tell me what he liked about it ... Success!

Cousin Cathy and I just chuckled as we watched God's good grace growing in those kids.

On the move again. After Sunday School, I ...

- took some time to visit on the way out of church,
- collected the flowers,
- drove home,
- fixed lunch for Harry and me,

- put the soup in the crockpot,
- figured out when I needed to put things in the oven,
- finished setting the table,
- pulled out the dishes and silverware,
- gave Harry a haircut, and
- greeted Mom and my brother, David, at 2:00 p.m.

David gave Harry a massage, while Mom and I …

- went into the computer room to look at pictures,
- scanned some slides into the computer for David,
- greeted Cousin Cathy at 3:30 p.m.,
- continued looking at pictures,
- greeted my sister-in-law, Trish, at 4:00 p.m., and
- answered the phone: two guests would be a little late.

We had a great dinner … not five, six, or eight (the number kept changing throughout the week) … but seven. We sat on the two living room sofas visiting while dishes came from the kitchen on small and medium plates:

- Shrimp Appetizers,
- Hamburger Cabbage over Brown Rice, and
- Greek Salad.

Then we moved to the table for a bowl of Split Pea Soup and finally, with everyone groaning at the thought of another course … we devoured Cream Cheese Brownies with Maraschino Cherries.

More visiting … everyone left happy.

After they were all gone, I …

- rinsed the dishes,
- loaded the dishwasher, and
- went downstairs to hang with Harry.

Harry pulled on my toes and rubbed my feet, threw a bath-robe over me, and ten minutes later, I conked out for one and one-half hours. And that was that! It took me three evenings to recover!

And That Was That!

The List

Birthdays are funny things. They're important to some people and not so important to others. Mom and David were the first ones to wish me a Happy Birthday … three days before it occurred.

When I got home from work on Wednesday, my birthday, I played my messages. First, my brother, Stephen, sang Happy Birthday, then Dick (Carol's husband), then my brother, Kevin. I was laughing and enjoying each one. Another brother, Charles, left a message saying if he'd gotten me in person, he would have sung me a song. (I wondered why he didn't … everyone else seemed to do it.) There were others who left messages … they all made The List.

Some people think I have a pre-planned list for checking people off, but I don't. I just start a list when people start wishing me a Happy Birthday and add the names as they go. (However, I DO mentally check off my family at the end of the day! So maybe there is an expectation after all.)

Here's what happened with Harry …

On the day before my birthday, Harry had forgotten to do the payroll. After dinner he went back to the office. I took off to visit a friend who was recovering from hip surgery. Then I ran to Costco and got a bunch of stuff to replenish our larder … including "mondo" chocolate cupcakes with buttercream icing.

I also got a new phone system to replace my failing one. Happy Birthday to me!

I got home at 8:20 p.m. Within ten minutes, we were eating a pre-birthday treat (cupcake surrounded by whipped cream). Both of us had the same reaction, but both of us waited until we finished our dessert before stating, "Next time we should just split one."

On Wednesday morning, I waited for Harry to wish me a Happy Birthday at breakfast ... and waited ... and waited.

When I got home, we hugged and kissed, as usual ... but no birthday greeting. He just shooed me upstairs to fix dinner. I enjoyed my messages and fixed dinner ... but still nothing. I got dessert (we split a birthday cupcake and smothered it with whipped cream to hide the cut marks) ... but still nothing. Ann, my sister-in-law, came over while we were watching TV ... with a gift and a card ... still nothing from Harry. I thought, "Maybe when we hit the hay." But bedtime came and went and yet again ... nothing.

The next day, I went to the office and asked the ladies I worked with to guess who didn't make The List. They guessed a few people but were shocked to find out it was Harry, their boss. That night we had a repetition of the previous night. I fixed dinner, and we watched a one-hour show. As we were starting another show, I asked him to put the TV on pause. I said, "Give me four words!"

Without hesitating, he replied, "I love you, Kate."

Well, who can argue with those four words? We went back to the show. After about ten minutes, as I was about to go upstairs to get ice, I said, "Give me four more words."

He stalled for a few seconds and then asked, "Why should I ... huh?"

It took me a couple of seconds to realize he had just given me four more words, so I left the room laughing. When I came back, I sat on the edge of my chair and leaned over facing him (like a cobra) saying, "Give me the four words you should have said yesterday."

Without hesitation he responded, "Happy Birthday to you."

"YOU MADE THE LIST!" I yelled as I left to get our dessert.

All was well in my world.

Big-Hair

I was so disgusted with Harry … he wouldn't say anything about my new haircut and "do." Here's what happened …

A month earlier, Mom and I had gone to the beauty parlor together. We both had gotten perms. She had her normal perm, and I had a spiral. Since then, I had been scrunching my wet hair with hair gel to get the curls to harden. It had been working well for me, but I kept thinking it would be good if I'd put it up once to see if I could look like Farrah Fawcett.

(Fast-forward ahead, one month.) Mom and I took the afternoon to go to the beauty parlor to get haircuts. While I was getting my hair cut, I mentioned that I hadn't put it up yet. My stylist asked if I wanted to have a set. Mom was having one, so I said, "Sure!" She put oodles of "product" in her palm, but I didn't say a word … I just let her do whatever she wanted to do. (If Harry or I were allergic to the smells, I'd just wash it out before bed.) She set my hair, which was about twelve inches long, and put me under the dryer. After drying, the rollers came out, hair was pulled and hair was teased. I knew I was in for a "Big-Hair" day.

Spray … Tease … Spray … Scrunch … Spray … I was looking pretty good. Before it was over, two stylists were working to ensure that my Big-Hair was also Shiny-Hair. My hair was bouncing around my face for the first time in years. We all wondered what Harry's reaction would be.

When Mom and I got back to her place, we sat outside and visited with my brother, David, for a while. He thought we both looked cute. After a while, I had to leave, which started another discussion about what Harry's reaction would be. Each of us had a different thought. I told them he might just say, "Feed me." (We'd been married for 30 years!)

All the way home from Woodland, I was thinking about one thing … my hair. At one point, a car pulled up in a sixty-mph zone on my right and paced me. I really wanted to move right, so after about ten seconds, I looked over at the other driver. She was looking directly at me! Then she sped up a little, and I had the opportunity to move over. "Gee, that was odd," I thought. I chalked it up to her noticing my Big-Hair. (I never did find out why she was staring at me.)

When I got home, I let Jud, our overly confident Labrador mix, out of the car. He bounded into the house to see Harry and his food dish, in some order. I came in to find Harry focusing his attention downward on petting Jud. When he finally looked at me, I was two feet away. I assumed I was in his blurry zone, but how can you miss Big-Hair? I was lucky to get a slight spark of recognition. Finally, I said, "Well, I guess I'll go get dinner started."

I went upstairs, started the meal, made the salad, set up the tripod, and snapped a few pictures. When I took dinner down to him, I handed him his plate with a one-second delay. He glanced at my "do," but still didn't say anything. We watched a TV show. I kept waiting for a reaction, but didn't get one. (It seemed to me if I took the trouble of getting a haircut, he should take the trouble to notice and comment!) Disgusted, after being home for two hours, I told him to put the TV on pause. Then I got down on my knees and edged over to him so that our heads were at the same height.

"Say something!" I demanded.

"That's one of the better one's you've had," he replied.

We laughed a little, and I stood to go back to my chair.

"Say something," he said.

"… I love you … Harry?" I responded, hesitantly. Then, realizing the symmetry of our questions, I asked "Did you get a haircut today?"

A faint smile played at the edge of his mouth. "Uh-huh," he mumbled as he nodded.

Oops!

PART THREE

TEA PARTIES

Prelude

It started innocently enough. My friend Carol had a death in the family. Her daughter-in-law had died leaving behind a distraught husband and two little girls, six and eight years old. Though I didn't really know the girls, I wondered if there was something I could do. Carol and I decided it would be fun to have a special little tea party.

We knew it would be important to have a fancy name to go with our special soiree. We settled on "The Ladies' Tea Party." It was a plain little name for the elegant party we were planning, but in the ensuing years, with "Second Annual," and eventually "Tenth Annual," tacked on the front of it, the Ladies' Tea Party became a thing of wonder … and mental gyrations!

I've never had children, but I've organized lots of parties and I've made lots of lists. I started with a few personal rules:

- The dishes, glasses, and silverware had to be tiny,
- The food had to be plentiful in case of picky eaters,
- The colors had to be varied and bright,
- The place settings had to be fine china, and
- The servings had to be individualized.

As I started ruminating over the menu, I got more and more excited. Cookbooks were flying off the top shelves. Cupboard doors, seldom opened, were thrown wide as all sorts of fancy little containers were pressed into service for the first time in their lives.

And so it began …

The Ladies' Tea Party

September 15, 1996

We had been planning the Ladies' Tea Party for about two months. Carol brought her two granddaughters, Stephanie (eight) and Brittany (six). Connie brought two of her granddaughters, Justine (six) and Chelsea (four). We all wore tea party dresses and visited and had a wonderful time. We had planned to picnic on the lawn out back, and play croquet, too, but our plans changed dramatically at the last minute, as you will soon see …

The menu and shopping list were taking shape and grew so large they had to be tamed before they could take on lives of their own.

Menu

Menu	
Lemon-Lime Punch	
Cashew Chicken Loaf	
Sandwiches	Peanut butter
	Peanut butter and honey mixed
	Raspberry jelly
Condiments	Black olives, Green olives
	Cucumber chips
	Cucumbers, Mustard
Fruit	Cantaloupe, Honeydew, Banana,
	Green grapes, Red grapes, Yogurt
Muffins	Carrot & Pineapple
Cheese	Cheese Ball & Crackers
Salad	Lettuce, red onion, green pepper,
	Water chestnuts, and tomato
Dessert	Lemon Bread, Orange Juice Petit Fours
Tea	Good Earth Original

Shopping List

2 ½ cups Chicken	Cucumber
½ cup cashews	Red Lettuce
½ cup Half & Half	Yogurt (Vanilla)
2 packages cream cheese	Champagne
Herbal Teas	Crackers
Orange Juice 6 oz (2)	Milk
Lemonade 6 oz	Broccoli
Pineapple Juice	Tomato
Grenadine Syrup	Green & Black Olives
Carbonated Lemon-Lime	Cucumber chips
Lemon Garnish	Whipping Cream
Peanut Butter	

Set Out
3 vases of flowers
Napkins
Silverware
Tables/Chairs/Cloths
Replacement Cloths
S&P Shakers
Tray (for fruit compotes)
Cucumbers/Paprika

The Setting

It hadn't really rained much that summer, but the weather report for the last week had been teasing about rain. The night before The Ladies' Tea Party it poured and poured. Since Harry and I were in the middle of remodeling the deck, we were ill-prepared for what we got. The tar paper layered on the bare plywood was only good enough for showers. Our deluge was way more than a shower. The water was streaming into the garage below the deck. It was bad. In fact, one of the three automatic garage doors was operating on its own about every half-hour! Now, isn't that a scary thought.

The outside was "out," we had to come in. The greenhouse was chosen as the "in" room. Having had a little forewarning of rain, I made sure the sunporch off the kitchen, which had always functioned as a greenhouse, was totally cleaned out. All the plants were freshened. Many more were brought in from the front porch. We had a beautiful jungle of glass and plants to wind through. The small metal table, paired with a green tablecloth, was perfect for the little girls. The card table with a green-patterned tablecloth did the trick for the three older ladies. It was an eight-foot by twenty-foot jungle. It threatened to be a little tight ... but dry!

A handcrafted birdhouse on a five-foot stand was right at home between the two tables. A fuzzy Chenille plant, in full bloom, was perched on the inside wall of the greenhouse. A Poor Man's Orchid from Harry's Mom, at the peak of its bloom, had a place of honor on a platform hanging from a beam holding up the glass roof. Several Coleus plants had been enjoying the humid summer and grew to a spectacular four feet high! The purple Wandering Jew was cascading down from the ceiling covering part of the entrance. It was colorful and dense. Ajax, our tame Orange-Winged Amazon parrot, had a perch of honor ... located in the greenery right next to the girls' table. (They didn't see him at first because the plants were so dense.)

Harry had set the CD player to do a continuous run of soft classical music, including Vivaldi, Mozart, Schumann, and Beethoven. Connie and Carol noticed and appreciated the music right away!

The Arrival

At 2:00 p.m., Connie, Justine, and Chelsea arrived bearing fresh roses from Connie's garden. The girls were wearing brand-new matching dark blue dresses from their sojourn to Clackamas Town Center the day before. They had picked out the dresses themselves. Rather than come right in, they wanted to stay outside awhile and play with the dogs. Bo, our German Shepherd, had a chance to romp with them a little and find out what "little girl" voices are all about.

Almost immediately, Carol came with Stephanie and Brittany bearing some art projects she had been saving for a rainy day. They were in shades of peach and pink floral.

Our Ladies' Tea Party had begun.

The Lunch Menu

The tables were dressed simply with floral napkins and forks. The first glimpse of the greenhouse was all about the plants. Trays of plates, glasses, and tea settings had been laid out in the kitchen: One tray for the luncheon session, the other for the tea session. The main course was served on pink glass plates for one table and silver-trimmed white plates for the other.

We started with a special version of Mimosa ... orange juice and sparkling apple cider for some ... orange juice and champagne for others. The Mimosas were served in small wine glasses for the little ladies, and tall wine glasses for the older ladies. All this took place in a room with a tile floor. Carol and Connie were more than little apprehensive, but the rule about using breakable place settings had been made clear early in the process and would not be changed!

Sandwiches, cheese muffins, fruit, and some tiny cheddar cheese crackers were the staples of the main course. The open-faced sandwiches had to be made at the last minute to ensure their freshness. There were three types. First, there were Peanut

Butter and Black Cherry Jam sandwiches on circles of Wonder Bread. (My friends had given me plenty of advice: Cathy made sure I had included "PB&J" on the menu; Marg suggested cookie cutters and opened faces.) The "PB&J" sandwiches looked pretty with a base of "PB" and a dollop of "J" in the center. The second type of sandwich was made with a tuna fish mixture and diced cucumber chips. It was served on a leaf of lettuce, sprinkled with some salted sunflower nuts, all on a base of a small, thin slice of sourdough bread. Finally, there were Cucumber Sandwiches on herb bread with mayonnaise, red lettuce and a thin slice of red onion topped by a paprika-covered slice of cucumber.

The rest of the menu received similar attention. Since cheese muffins taste best if they're warm, they went into the oven at about 1:45 p.m.

The fruit was served in cut glass hors d'oeuvres dishes, one per table. Large plump green seedless grapes, cut-up melons and cut-up pineapple in a tri-sectioned dish, with a little silver fork, graced the little girls' table. Tiny individual salt and pepper shakers were at each table. The Cheddar Crackers were served in a small stainless-steel sugar bowl. It was a perfect size for the little table.

The Meal

The girls were very adult (and evidently very hungry). The PB&J sandwiches were a hit. They were gone in the blink of an eye. The cheese muffins didn't last very long either. After topping off the meal with assorted fruits, I heard some "I'm full" comments, but the crackers had yet to be munched. Naturally,

Thompson grapes and Cheddar Crackers also found their way to furry little mouths as four West Highland White Terriers (Tori, Molly, Chatterbox and Sara) and even Ajax, the parrot, reaped the benefit of our Tea Party fare. All the animals were on their best behavior. They were all food-oriented … it wasn't a stretch.

The Craft

After lunch, we went into the living room and did some coloring at the glass table, with colored pencils. Those of us who weren't coloring at the time either played with some magnets on the coffee table, or had more Mimosa (depending on how many digits they had in their age). And then, as hoped, things started to get out of control.

After rounding up a pair of scissors and glue holders, the girls started making little dolls out of felt and popsicle sticks. When I went downstairs to get a second pair of scissors, Chelsea wanted to know what was downstairs.

"Only our bedroom," I replied.

Then she wanted to know if she could go downstairs.

"Sure."

All the girls went down with me. When we got there, I found myself forty years younger: the girls were opening and closing every door and cupboard they could find.

Justine had been the first downstairs and went straight down the hall, looped to the right through the bathroom, and showed up in front of us as we entered the bedroom. The others were so excited about her appearance from out of the blue, they all wanted to know how she did it. She willingly led a merry chase. After four screaming, giggling loops, ... and the bathroom door bumper going sproing, Sproing, SPROING! ... I thought it might be best if we returned to the party just in case the noise might be getting on anyone's nerves ... like mine.

When we got back upstairs, it was pretty clear everyone was still excited, especially Ajax, who chose to do a little singing ... at the top of his little lungs. We joined him in singing a song, but a smidge of that goes a long, long way in a house with tile floors and minimal carpets. We all calmed down instantly as the craft-making began in earnest.

The Tea

Sugar is not the best thing in the world, and I had two personal rules to follow: it had to come in small amounts, and it had to be dressed up with little plates and lots of breakable heirlooms. Since the Tea Menu was built around sugary treats, the cookies had to be lightweight, thin, and plentiful. We had homemade Orange Butter Cookies (the homemade part really wowed Stephanie). They had been pressed flat with a "tool" before baking. We had cute little Swedish Ginger Thins which were shaped like a daisy. They were half as thick as the Orange Butter Cookies. We also had some modest-sized Cinnamon Graham Stars. The tea itself was Good Earth Original ... very sweet but without sugar!

Brittany cornered me in the kitchen. She didn't think she wanted any tea, and I made sure she knew it was fine with me. I suggested she could have some lemonade. That was fine with her. Of course, I remarked the tea would be served in tiny flowery demitasse cups, each with a real gold rim, and if it didn't taste just right, she could always add some sugar and cream from the miniature glass sugar set, with a tiny pewter Irish spoon. Throughout the explanation, my hand was waving over all the breakables on the counter. Brittany's eyes got bigger and bigger. She didn't take too long to decide she would try some tea after all.

The girls were beside themselves when they found out it was time for the cookies. Carol and Connie made sure they understood no one would eat anything until we had both of the tables all set up for the tea. With the four little girls in their places, we transformed the bare tables into a fairy land of china and goodies.

Stephanie showed her three companions how to drink with their pinky fingers raised. Tea was poured from a china teapot and left on their table. Sugar and cream were passed around. The little Irish spoon accidentally found its way into the first little cup of tea but was soon resurrected, wiped, and passed on to the next person. That happened with each little girl, as the older ladies watched from afar, rolling their eyes. The serving platter with the cookies was in its place, the china plates were waiting in front of each girl and all the tea had been served. The sugar portion of the Tea Party began!

As Carol, Connie, and I were pouring our own tea, we noticed the plate at the next table was just about empty. (Not a whole lot of time elapsed between these two paragraphs.) But we also noticed we'd accidentally left the sugar and creamer on their table, so I rose and asked the girls if they'd like a few more cookies. Of course, they said "Yeesss!" I told them I'd take the opportunity to remove the Sugar and Creamer set.

After Brittany had just a "tad" more cream, the switch took place. And the Tea Party continued. The goodies were so magical the dogs didn't get any ... even though they were present, just in case!

The Aftermath

While we finished our tea, the girls finished their crafts in the living room. Before they left, they all got a chance to hold and pet the parrot. There were smiles all around. Two or three colorful tailfeathers (not freshly pulled) were in everyone's hands, and by about 5:00 p.m., there were lots of hugs and waving goodbye. All in all, it was a fairly tame Tea Party, probably because everyone was dressed up. That changed dramatically in subsequent years.

The Second Annual Ladies' Tea Party

August 9, 1997

Harry scheduled his day around the Tea Party. I can just imagine him thinking, "What can I do to keep me away from the house while all the Tea-Party people are here?"

The Guest List

This year, the guest list never really settled down until the last minute ... the very last minute! I knew Carol and Connie would be bringing their granddaughters, but I didn't know exactly how many others were coming. We had such an easy time of it the first year that I sent out a lot more invitations. There were fourteen people expected after the first round of RSVPs. A few weeks later, the expected attendance dropped to twelve. A few days later it was down to nine. An hour before the expected arrival, we were back up to eleven. When everyone showed up, we had a full thirteen people ... and I ended up totally baffled!

The Preparation

Since the guest list kept changing every time I turned around, I made a decision about two days before the party: prepare for the possibility of having twelve people. I set out twelve of everything: Crystal, Silver, Napkins, Dinner plates, Dessert plates, and Chairs.

On the day of the party, the weather report assured me of a sunny day. Knowing there were probably only nine people coming, I set up three tables on the lawn in the backyard. I knew I could make adjustments at the last minute, if necessary. But, as you'll soon see, I did get a bit bewildered and almost lost it. First, let's step back just a bit and see how the guest list actually changed during the month. (In the table, my girlfriends are listed in bold.)

Name	Relationship	Age	Prior to Tea Time				Tea Time
			1 month	1 week	1 day	1 hour	
Kathy	That's me	adult	1	1	1	1	1
Carol	Long-time friend	adult	1	1	1	1	1
Janet	Daughter	adult	1				1
Stephanie	Granddaughter	9	1				1
Brittany	Granddaughter	7	1	1	1	1	1
Connie	Long-time friend	adult	1	1	1	1	1
Mom	Mother	adult		1			
Emma	Niece	7		1	1	1	1
Traci	Granddaughter	10	1	1	1	1	1
Justine	Granddaughter	7	1	1	1	1	1
Chelsea	Granddaughter	5	1	1	1	1	1
Kimberly	Granddaughter	3	1	1	1	1	1
Marg	Long-time friend	adult	1	1		1	1
Mary Jo	Daughter-in-law	adult				1	1
Katie	Granddaughter	12	1	1			
Cathy	Long-time friend	adult	1				
Lexie	Neighbor	3	1				
Total			14	12	9	11	13
Adults			6	5	3	5	6
Children			8	7	6	6	7
Westies			4	4	3	4	4

The Setting

Harry and his brother Jon had been working on the site development for the new barn. (Well, it wasn't exactly a barn. It was a large workshop ... but who can remember to say "workshop" when "barn" just rolls off the tongue.) Work was progressing nicely during the week before the party. Unfortunately, this resulted in a major construction site, complete with stacks of lumber, as a greeting area for the Ladies' Tea Party. To set off the two worlds, I used quite a number of potted plants as a barricade between reality and fantasy. Since it was Saturday, there was no work effort on the barn ... thankfully, all was quiet!

We had a lush green lawn for our locale with thanks to Harry for three months of fertilizing and mowing. New hangers, arching out from tree trunks, displayed baskets of pink begonias, trailing lobelia, Wandering Jew, and impatiens. Pots of light blue petunias softened one boundary of the croquet area. A tall pot of calla lilies stood sentinel over one of the wickets to keep it from accidentally tripping a guest. A large potted fir provided a visual screen to keep the younger ladies from slipping down the slope into the terraced portion of the yard.

Mimosas again ... don't mess with a good thing. Grandma Beaucage's crystal goblets were set out for older ladies, while glass champagne goblets held some nectar for the little ladies. Grandma's Fine China, a little chipped for its 100 years of wear, showed pretty little pink rosebuds against the backdrop of light blue tablecloths. White paper napkins and forks completed the settings. The centerpieces were three four-inch terracotta pots with a plaid design, each planted with a silk sunflower in a foam base disguised with sphagnum moss. They were made about three months earlier in anticipation of the event.

The Final Preparation

Everything was on schedule. Guests were due to arrive at 1:00 p.m. My timetable indicated I should start making the quiche at noon. At that moment, Marg called to see if she and her daughter-in-law, Mary Jo, could still come.

"That will be wonderful!"

Back up to eleven guests. I made the quiche and positioned eleven tomato slices on the nine-inch-square pan of quiche batter, dusting everything generously with one-half cup of Parmesan cheese. The tomato slices would be helpful at the last minute when cutting the quiche. A platter of lettuce beds was readied to assist in serving the quiche. And finally, it was time to make the sandwiches. It seemed I was about five minutes behind schedule with no chance to make it up.

The Arrival

At 1:00 p.m. exactly, all hell broke loose: Gary and Connie arrived in two cars with their five charges, ages three to ten. The dogs started barking ... "Arp, Arp, Arp!" The persistent alarm on the oven announced the Parmesan Quiche had finished its 45-minute sojourn in the oven ... "Beep - Beep - Beep!" Emma, age seven, entered the kitchen and demanded ... "What STINKS?"... Gary turned gray and melted into the door frame as the commotion showed no signs of diminishing ... "Arp, Arp, Arp!" ... "Beep - Beep - Beep!" ... "Arp, Arp, Arp!" ... "What

STINKS?" Marg was pouring the beverages. She offered Gary some champagne. He tossed it down in record time. Before we knew it, he was already driving out toward the cul-de-sac for the three-block trip home. The adult ladies looked at each other with eyebrows raised and shoulders shrugged as we whispered, "Goodbye, Gary."

At 1:05 p.m. exactly, the timer and Emma had subsided, but the dogs were still going strong … "Arp, Arp, Arp!" … greeting Carol and her granddaughters as they drove up. I went out to greet Carol and Brittany and was thrilled to see that Janet (Carol's daughter) and Stephanie were able to come after all. "Aunt Jan" and the girls had brought a little gift sack of treats fit for a tea party, including some little dog biscuits for the furry four-legged girls. I had only been expecting Carol and Brittany in Carol's car. A few mental gyrations later and I was thanking my lucky stars I had set out twelve of everything. With a few quick movements in the kitchen, I now had thirteen of everything … or so I thought.

The Menu and the Party

The gathering began with Mimosas for everyone: "with" for the older ladies, "without" for the little ladies. We all strolled outside and enjoyed the surroundings (the dogs were still a little agitated because of all the commotion).

Just before we began our brunch, the adults paraded out with plates, bowls, and platters of food.

"Sit down," I invited.

Since the quiche (in individual lettuce beds) was the only hot food, I served it myself from a large china platter. Before I finished serving the second table, there was a little hubbub at the third table. I went right over there and served them, but when I got to Emma, I reminded her this was the dish she had smelled when she arrived, and asked if I could serve her a piece? She politely said, "No, thank you." With an odd number of attendees, and an odd number of quiche servings, I wasn't surprised to return the platter to the kitchen with one piece left over.

Finally, all were seated, staring at a feast which included:

- Light and cheesy quiche,

- Three kinds of sandwiches,

- Thin slices of turkey rolled around cream cheese,

- Three dishes of colorful Carmen-Miranda fruit, and

- Connie's large platter of pumpkin bread sticks.

The Predicament

As I was sitting down, Connie exclaimed, "Kathy, I don't have any quiche." I apologized and darted off into the house to get the last portion of quiche. I wasn't sure what had gone wrong.

- Didn't I have an odd number of guests?

- Emma declined her piece.

- Shouldn't there have been an even number served?

- Shouldn't there be one piece left over?

What had gone wrong? There wasn't time to think it through. On the way back outside with Connie's plate of quiche, I started doing the mental math from the other direction:

- There should have been thirteen guests.

- Emma didn't have any quiche.

- Twelve guests should be eating quiche.

- An odd number of tomatoes topped the quiche.

- The quiche was cut according to the tomatoes.

Oh, my goodness! There were only eleven slices of tomato to start with. Oh, no, that must mean: *There was one more guest who didn't get quiche!* Who was it?!!!

As I set Connie's plate in front of her, I noticed Justine (seven) didn't have any quiche. "Justine," I exclaimed, forcing myself to stay calm. "You didn't get any quiche! Would you like some, Sweetheart?"

"No-thank-you," she replied, rushing through the words.

"Are you sure?" I queried once more, stretching out my words. "There's plenty." I had lied but was pleased with myself for not choking on the words.

"No, thank you," she replied once more.

I dodged a bullet! Gratefully, I sat down and *knew* I was going to have a good time at the party. We enjoyed our food, the flowers, the temperate weather, and the gathering. Everyone ate in grand fashion as though we were wearing wide-brimmed plumed hats with parasols at our sides.

The Nip

After we had our brunch, the girls got a little restless. Justine jumped up and started roaming around the croquet area. Then she started dancing. Molly, of course, is not a dancer. She's just a little terrier whose only strenuous activity is being "tortured" by Harry and Kate. She didn't really get into this dancing stuff. Then Justine, who was unable to coax the other girls from their chairs by dancing, went on to jumping. Molly, who evidently had a short fuse, had had it! She darted over to Justine and nipped her in the calf. That seemed to her to be an effective way of stopping this jumping stuff. Justine let out a yelp, and everyone, especially me, turned with shocked faces. Justine was quite upset. Her recovery came pretty fast when Connie dried her eyes and found there was no blood … she just experienced a pinch … but a healthy pinch, at that.

The Croquet

And so, we finished the lunch and went on to start up a round of croquet. As the games began, three of the six adults and one of the Westies begged their leave. By this time, it was pretty warm outside. Connie and I cooled off in the kitchen on the pretense of rinsing and stacking the plates, crystal, and silver. Meanwhile, Carol had her hands full corralling seven little girls with their six croquet balls and mallets who had never heard of croquet. Before we could finish inside, a two-person entourage, Traci and Emma, came through asking if they could tour the house on their own. It seemed okay to us, so off they went, exploring the basement and the garage. Traci stopped to try on

Harry's big gardening hat and then discovered a swinging macrame chair on the lower patio.

Meanwhile, as Connie and I arrived outside, Carol turned to us with the look of an abandoned grandmother of who wasn't used to watching over seven little charges who were playing "golf" with croquet equipment. AAWK! If you're trying to formulate a picture of us, imagine three women in their fifties, with the palms of our hands slapping our cheeks, our mouths dropping open, our coifed curls drooping, and our eyes bugging out ... it was Munch's Scream all over again. We were out of our element ... but back to the game: We made up the croquet rules as we went along ... with an eye out for the younger girls being able to keep up with the older ones. Everything seemed to be falling into place. We were sitting at one of the tables resting peacefully when suddenly Connie realized there was a reason it was so restful ... five of the girls had disappeared!

The Jilt

And so, Connie hustled off in the direction they were last seen. At the same time, Harry had run out of things to do and had returned home early. Anxious to keep his Tea Party attendance to a minimum, he jumped on the ride-on lawn mower and started out of the garage. The five little girls were gathered around him chattily asking what he was doing here. "I own this place," he replied, abruptly. Then down the hill he went on his mower at top speed, and whistled over his shoulder for Bo to join him ... leaving the little girls in a befuddled state at the top of the hill ... where Connie found them.

Harry and Bo Beat Feet

The Tea

Off in another world, Chelsea (five) and Kimberly (three) helped me prepare the herb tea. Emma came in and thanked me for the invitation to have some tea, but she didn't believe she cared for any tea. "Okay," I said with a smile. But when we went outdoors, I gave her a cup anyway ... the little floral demitasse cup with gold trim ... saying it would balance the look of the table. The tiny glass sugar bowl and creamer was set out, too. Two plates of sugar cookies of different shapes and colors adorned each table. There were Lemon Crispies, Oatmeal Pecan cookies, Brownies, and Stained-Glass Cookies

(Grandma Walsh's recipe using white chocolate with colored marshmallows, sliced very thin).

The six older girls sat around one table leaving the three adults and little Kimberly to another table. The tea, being iced to counteract the heat of the day, made a huge hit with everyone, including Emma. (She had decided she'd have some tea after all because she liked iced tea.) However, the biggest thrill of all was seeing the girls become fast friends while sharing their desserts. It made me think of the magic about to happen in a few short years as they would all turn into graceful swans (sooner than any of us expected).

The Flowers at the End

After three hours, finishing with a lot of sweet tea and sugar, it was time to load everyone into the cars for the trip home. Each of the girls was surprised with a centerpiece. We took plenty of pictures of happy faces, plaid flowerpots, and silk sunflowers. Stephanie exchanged addresses with Traci and Emma, and everyone got into hugging. Two tired adults loaded their seven little girls and the one visiting Westie into two cars. They drove off leaving one tired adult waving goodbye with a very satisfied smile on her face. (Molly too was satisfied ... but for a totally different reason.)

Cranky Molly

As of 2021, it has been 24 years since the Second Annual Ladies' Tea Party … and Carol is still recounting her abandonment issues!

The Third Annual Ladies' Tea Party

August 23, 1998

T he Ladies' Tea Party came at the same time as Harry's family reunion, my retirement party in Spokane, and the starting of a new business. It was a wonderful party, but I ran out of energy for summarizing it. A year later, I picked up the pieces.

As I looked back through my notes, I discovered only one note on my to-do list for Saturday, August 22: Find the teacups! I didn't know they were missing.

I went to a year-old shopping list already started on the computer.

Shopping List	
Orange Juice	Lettuce
Cookie Cutter	Cupcakes
Peanut Butter	Tea
Honey	Sugar
Jams	Cream
Napkins, Forks, Plates	Brushes
Tuna	Cheeses Spread
Pecans	Champagne

I also found a sketch of what I expected the luncheon and the tea phases to look like so I'd have the right plates and utensils ready, but since a Tea Party is more about mood than ritual, I ditched the sketch and the notes. New ideas were forming fast.

The Rush

I can't remember why, but I do know I was running fashionably late. Carol and her daughter, Janet, arrived with Stephanie and Brittany. Mercifully, they weren't early. Connie came with Traci, Justine, Chelsea, and Kimberly. Since I was running late, I hadn't finished fixing the sandwiches. I tackled the tuna sandwiches while Carol helped the girls get settled in. Per Carol's brilliant suggestion, the peanut butter sandwiches were left for the girls to make.

The Icebreaker

There are always a few awkward moments when the little girls get together, which is compounded by a structured sipping of mimosa. There's not a lot you can do about that except work through it until everyone gets to know each other. But this year, while I was working on the tuna sandwiches, one of the girls found a quart bucket of buttons (which I hadn't put away … Oops). They were thrilled with the buttons and wanted to make some jewelry, so we pulled out the breadboard and got out the string and some blunt scissors. Everyone got lost in the moment of buttoning. Precious buttons became necklaces, strings of pearls, bracelets, and even rings. By the time we were ready to have our mimosa, they were all long-lost friends.

Unusual Palettes

With the breadboard still as the center of attention, out came the cookie cutters. Everyone under twelve years of age stamped circles and bears from Wonder Bread slices and spread them with peanut butter and jam … and honey … and mustard … and sweet pickles … and olives … and mayonnaise. It was a thing of beauty to see the smallest of the girls on her toes trying to look at the offerings on the breadboard. The end results looked pretty awful, but whatever the girls made, they ate. I think there might be a lesson in that.

Acrylic Paints

Connie brought some plain wooden birdhouses and some acrylic paints. Between lunch and tea, we all gathered around the metal table on the deck and had a wonderful time decorating our birdhouses. The younger girls went for glitz, while the older girls painted with some plan in mind. "Aunt Jan" was buzzing around helping the girls with their projects.

A few paint spots got on the metal table. After a year, they were still there, a sweet reminder of a fun party. (Maybe when I have to spray the table, again, I'll leave one or two of the spots untouched.) Spots on the clothes, deck covering, arms, and dogs were minimal. After our tea, everyone gathered for pictures … with their birdhouses and their new jewelry. What a nice memory!

Painted Whirligigs and Birdhouses

The Fourth Annual Ladies' Tea Party

September 12, 1999

The 1999 Ladies' Tea Party started in a most unusual way. I had already done the shopping, but the menu was still on scratch paper. I knew I had to get it formalized or I'd be winging it all through the party. Not a good plan! At about 11:10 a.m. I sat down at the computer and started building a table of menu items. All of a sudden, the computer rebooted on its own. The only other time it had rebooted by itself was when I had a diskette in the drive. There was nothing like a diskette in any of the drives. I wondered if there was a late-breaking 9/9/99 virus I had contracted. At any rate, I restarted my document and typed the menu, assigned times, saved, and printed everything. Knowing I only had one-half hour before I had to get the food ready, I finished tidying up the yard and set the table. When I returned to the house at about 11:35 a.m., I noticed the power was out! I still hadn't baked the quiche, nor had I baked the muffins. Was this an impending disaster?

Alternatives

My neighbor Dorothy walked by with some other neighbors, did a little walk-through of our Tea Party area, and suggested I bake the quiche in the trailer. What a great idea ... a real life-saver. I had a little trouble locating the keys, but I knew they were in the basement closet. (It was the only room in the house with no window.) Fortunately, as I fumbled around in the pitch-black atmosphere, I remembered exactly where in that closet I had placed them. Once inside the trailer, I tried to start the oven, but the gas wasn't turned on. Not being comfortable with the hook-ups, I thought about calling Harry but decided against the idea. Harry's no fool ... he had scurried away to the office to study his continuing education courses ... for the duration of the Tea Party! I was really in a pickle. The whole timetable was shot. I decided to make the sandwiches and take my shower. Things got better: The power came back on at 12:51 p.m. ... a full nine minutes before my guests were due to arrive. I quickly started the quiche and set the timer. The green salad was next ... thank goodness for my computer printout. I still had not prepared the fruit compote, nor the crackers and cheese. What a relief to find out the girls were thrilled to help prepare the meal!

The Arrivals

Carol and Brittany arrived first, in matching blue ensembles. Within minutes, Gary and Connie arrived. Gary stayed! He was the first man ever to attend a Ladies' Tea Party! They brought Traci, Justine, Chelsea, and Kimberly. Sara (a Westie), of course, is a regular at the Teas. I contributed two more Westies, Molly and Chatterbox, who by their very presence, seemed to terrify some of the guests. Oh, well, a few breadcrumbs tossed into willing mouths and all the dogs were under control. I also contributed Boris, our young African Gray parrot, who was quite content to witness the commotion from the security of his cage. Boris refused to talk, but he entertained everyone by raising and lowering the door to his cage with his beak and threatening to come out.

Janet, for some reason, couldn't make it this year. Perhaps it was because Jenae, her daughter, was all of four months!

No More Nips

Before anything else, we had to make sure there were no "nips" at this year's Ladies' Tea. I showed Justine (last year's "nippee") where the breadcrumbs were. Then I showed her how to feed a small piece to Molly (last year's "nipper") without losing a fingertip. Justine and Molly really got the hang of it. Crumb games kept Molly preoccupied while everyone else arrived and settled in.

Little Helpers

Melon balls were first on the list. Traci helped make honeydew balls. Chelsea made cantaloupe balls. Brittany made some delicate strips from the Crenshaw melon and Justine made similar strips from the other half of the honeydew melon. Chelsea cut the Starfruit. Traci prepared a platter of "Cheddar spray on Wheat Thins." By that time, we were all hungry for a nibble.

Teamwork

If we wanted to proceed with our Tea Party, we had to do it fast before we started to swoon from hunger. We quickly put together an assembly line to make the Fruit Compote in Grandma's crystal goblets:

- Justine put a serving of applesauce in each goblet,
- Chelsea and Brittany added melon balls and strips,

- Brittany placed exactly four grapes in each goblet,
- Traci added a spoonful of granola,
- Chelsea positioned a slice of Starfruit to the side, and
- I put on whipped cream and a maraschino cherry.

By that time, the house had really started to heat up. I think the innards of the thermostat must have taken a left turn during the power outage. (Before the party was over the house had passed 82 degrees … and was still climbing!)

With all the compote preparations complete, it was time to begin our Mimosa phase. (Gary cheated on the Mimosa by skipping the orange juice.) Traci passed the platter of crackers with cheese flowerets and we enjoyed catching up and finding out how the girls were liking school.

It was clear we were getting hungry. The girls started making their sandwiches. Peanut Butter and Strawberry Jam were the most popular. A new tool, which crimps two pieces of bread together, was a big hit! As we doctored up the sandwiches, I surmised this would be a pretty sane year. Then, within moments of that thought, I saw the sandwiches being adorned with whipping cream, black olives, and multiple maraschino cherries. It was a normal year, after all!

Special Request

Kimberly, who is four, spent the sandwich-making time, curled up on the loveseat next to Connie. She was pulling her feet up on the sofa … so the dogs couldn't get her. I didn't want her to miss out. Here's how the conversation went:

"Kimberly, would you like to make a sandwich?"

"Uh-uh."

"Would you like me to make a sandwich for you?"

"Uh-huh."

"Would you like some peanut butter and strawberry jam?"

"No."

"How about peanut butter and yummy orange marmalade?"

"No."

"Plain peanut butter?"

She shook her head.

"Just some strawberry jam?"

Again, she shook her head.

"Oh ... how about a 'butter' sandwich?"

"Uh-huh."

"A 'butter' sandwich it is, then!"

Since a butter sandwich was unlikely to provide the proper nutrients for a growing four-year-old, we made sure we had her favorite food on hand ... black olives. I knew I didn't have any in the pantry, so while one person made Kimberly a special butter sandwich, the rest of us went out to the trailer in search of black olives. We succeeded!

The Luncheon

The quiche was ready, the fruit compotes were ready, both the crimped and the cucumber sandwiches were ready, (the muffins were a hazard of the power outage and were never given another thought), and although the salad was ready, no one could agree on a salad dressing. Traci brushed off the table cloths and we rushed the food and table settings outside. Grandma's Fine China ... plates, dishes, platters, and saucers ... were a recognized tradition. Even with the procession from the house, down the new flagstone path, across the grass to the table with three dogs underfoot, there were no mishaps ... though none were expected.

We had a pleasant lunch. Gary liked the quiche. Kimberly had no less than ten black olives on her plate ... and ate them all. Another round of cheese and crackers prepared by Justine disappeared instantly. Surprisingly, the chicken and cucumber "spinner" sandwiches (held in place with a colored toothpick) were a hit with all members of the entourage.

Boris Attends the Tea Party

The Hidden Path

Just before the girls got up from the table, Justine remarked Molly seemed to obey her commands pretty well! And then they were up and off. This was the first year the girls found the little side trail from the Backyard to the Forest. Following Brittany, they wound their way through the woods, bumped into the fence, made their way around a dead branch (I wished I had removed it), and finally burst through to the other side. One by one, they came running around in a wide loop to the

Backyard entrance happy with their successful "woodswom-en-ship." Sara, the Westie, "got lost" in the Maid's Garden (a twenty-foot by twenty-foot bed of ivy featuring two azalea bushes surrounded by fir trees) but was soon recovered by a very young, concerned guest. Molly and Chatterbox continued terrorizing Kimberly by lying passively at my feet under the picnic table.

An Unexpected Visitor

We were very fortunate we didn't have needles raining on us during the meal. We were also fortunate the yellow jackets didn't discover our little party until we had finished eating. The arrival of a yellow jacket who was enamored with Brittany's last bit of quiche signaled the end of the third phase of the Fourth Annual Ladies' Tea Party. With very little effort, we cleared the table and brought everything back into the kitchen.

Getting Crafty

As the temperature rose in the house, Connie and I fought to see who would get to do the dishes while Carol helped the little ladies discover the joys of cross-stitching. Everyone seemed to get the hang of the running stitch around the edge, but when it came to actually tackling the design in the center, we began to realize this was a project that would take hours and was perhaps a little harder than we first thought! We soon discovered it was very important for the older girls to be helped by someone they were not related to. Kimberly sat on the sofa next to Grandpa Gary who helped her with her cross-stitch project. After about twenty minutes of struggling with the kits, Connie jumped up and announced Traci had to leave to catch her train to Chehalis. Traci is in eighth grade and has a beautiful smile and excellent manners. Lest she miss out on the essence of the Tea Party (sweets, that is), we snatched a paper plate, piled it with pie and cookies and a fork, wrapped it and sent her on her way with Gary.

Sweet and Sticky

It was now time for the final phase of the Ladies' Tea. As the girls packed up their projects, Carol helped with some of the cleanup. She was looking for a cloth to wipe the sticky jam jars from our earlier preparations. We finally looked at each other, shrugged, and decided the best thing to do was run the whole jar under the faucet. (I was grateful to live in a corner of the world where water is not a scarce commodity.)

We were all comfortable indoors, with the exception of the heat, which climbed another degree despite efforts to direct it downward. We elected to have our tea indoors. The four older girls took the glass-topped table as Carol, Connie, and I settled in on the sofas. We put out a sugar and creamer set, which was the same size as the demitasse teacups. The Chocolate Dream Pie was a big hit; the thin tea cookies are always a favorite. It seems Carol had gotten wise to the amount of sugar that is acceptable for the girls, so their platter was small and limited to eight cookies. But no one complained, nor did they look for more cookies. They did, however, want some more tea. Justine poured. After everyone had gone for the day, I was surprised (but shouldn't have been) to find all the sugar and cream were gone, too! And yet another Ladies' Tea Party came to an end!

Timetable

After everyone had left, I picked up my timetable ... developed, in theory, to help me get everything done before company came ... and filled in the actual times things got done. In some cases, I was almost an hour off schedule. Thank goodness for willing helpers.

Planned	Actual	
12:15	Not	Muffins
12:30	1:25	Fruit Compote: Applesauce, Melons, Grapes, Granola, Whipped Cream, Starfruit, Cherry
12:30	12:55	Quiche: Bacon & Swiss with Spinach
12:45	1:30	Crackers with cheese
12:50	1:00	Green Salad: Lettuce, red peppers, onion, water chestnuts, walnuts
1:00	1:40	OJ & Champagne; OJ & Cider

Follow-up on the Heat Problem

Afterward, when Harry and I got a chance to discuss the air conditioning, he showed me a special switch on the outside of the house. For some reason, the box had been opened. We didn't know if this was really the cause of the problem, but he wiggled the switch out and in, and by doing so, and performing some other relay-box gyrations, the heat pump finally kicked in and the house started cooling down. Very strange ... very strange, indeed!

The Fifth Annual Ladies' Tea Party

September, 2000

O ne would think after four Ladies' Tea Parties there would be no surprises, no disasters ... one would be wrong.

It started the night before the party. There were things to do to prepare for the special event. There was bread to make in my Valtrompia bread tins, so the bread slices would be in the shape of a star, a heart, or a daisy. There was a special frozen salad to make ... with orange juice concentrate as a base and maraschino cherries for visual appeal. Bananas and pineapple blended into the mixture kept it all together when it was frozen. Ginger Ale gave it an extra little sparkle. Grandma's recipe for chocolate wafer cookies, layered with whipping cream, frozen and sliced on the diagonal, resulted in a pretty striped dessert. Just about everything was ready. Only a few things were left for the day of the Tea Party: cheese and crackers, quiche, melon balls for the salad, cucumber sandwiches, and condiments. It was safe to retire knowing everything would be easily prepared the next morning.

The Next Morning's Set-Up

It was raining ... or threatening to rain!

There was no room for indecision. The Tea Party had to be held indoors. If we were lucky, we'd be able to have an outing, but the critical food portion had to be set up indoors. The sofas had to be moved to create a cozy ambience and also to make room for the tables. I was expecting seven girls and four adults. The girls' tables had to have matching tablecloths. First one, then two, finally three tables ... all were assembled with china and crystal. This was the first time I had set up tables in the living room. I stood back to admire them. Then I realized if there were spills, they'd stain the carpet. I got back into action. First one, then two, finally three tables ... all were disassembled, moved, and reassembled in a better location. Was it really better to have those tables over the tile floor ... not sure!

The counters were miraculously clean, the quiche was baked, the melon balls were scooped, and the drinks were chilled. Things were starting to look like a Tea Party by noon.

Everything was running smoothly until a crucial decision had to be made. The salad had to be removed from the freezer one hour before serving. I had a dilemma: should I remove the salad at 1:00 p.m. even though it might be two hours before it was served, or should I risk getting distracted and forget to thaw it at all? Early thawing won the toss, and the salad came out of the freezer. After all, frozen salads are fine even if they're completely thawed, aren't they? ... I was hopeful!

The Arrival

Connie brought Traci, Justine, Chelsea, Kimberly, and Breanna. The girls' mother, Michelle, came for good measure. Carol brought Stephanie and Brittany. Janet brought Jenae, who loved the bird and Molly.

As everyone came in, we got re-acquainted with each other. Nylons, pretty clothes, smiles, and happiness abounded. Crystal goblets appeared and a very special "cheese glass" came out for Breanna (two years old). The texture of the glass made it appear to be decorated with imaginary jewels. She was the only one to have such a special glass. (It takes a lot of effort to break one of those glasses.)

The Luncheon - Tempting Fate and Going with the Flow

Oops! The drinks and the shaky card tables weren't compatible, so out came a couple of towels. (I was glad I had repositioned the tables!) I never quite knew what happened because the person with the offending drink took the towel and cleaned up as necessary. By now, all the girls had found their places at the tables and the older ladies had settled on the sofa for a chat. The youngest girls were invited to come over and visit, as well. We shared some hors d'oeuvres, enjoyed the conversation, and caught up on all the events of the last year.

Kimberly was quite the little helper. She went into the kitchen, made an extra plate of crackers, and brought it back to the living room on Grandma's Fine China Serving Tray. She didn't even miss a beat on the step from the kitchen down into the living room. We had tempted fate … and won!

After a suitable length of time for visiting, the girls made themselves peanut butter and jelly sandwiches. We had squeeze dispensers for peanut butter and strawberry jam making clean-up a little easier than in the past. Everyone got to choose cookie cutters for the shape of their bread for sandwiches. The older ladies had the daises, which looked quite smart with cucumber rounds atop lettuce and mayonnaise. We were all enjoying our sandwiches when the younger ladies decided two sandwiches wouldn't quite fill them up. They departed en masse to the kitchen to make cucumber sandwiches for themselves. Evidently the girls must have been growing up fast because the cucumber sandwiches were a hit with everyone!

Not knowing if this would be a good year for a quiche, we had one that was sure to appeal to the older ladies. To avoid any opportunity for a miscount, the quiche was cut into fifteen pieces, even though there were only eleven of us. (In the end, the sandwiches were the most popular while only about half of the quiche was consumed.) The luncheon plate was not complete with just a quiche. The frozen salad would make a beautiful, orange complement to the vegetable quiche.

Oops! The frozen salad had been left out on the counter for a little longer than the requisite hour. No longer was it possible to dispense it with a flat spatula. I needed a large spoon for the deed, taking care to scoop from the center of the dish, rather than the liquefied sides. A few condiments finished the décor, including sweet or dill pickles and black or green. Something for everyone. At last, all were served and seated.

Oops, again! The melon balls, meant to complement the colors on the plate, had been overlooked. Another little helper got the melon balls from the refrigerator and passed them around ensuring each person had three melon balls on her plate.

As we began our luncheon, the frozen salad, which by that time had been out of the freezer for at least two hours, was creeping toward the edges of eleven plates, but it's not proper to fuss during a Tea Party, so that just had to be overlooked with a prayer. (Later, I noticed every plate returning to the kitchen was a little soupy … lesson learned!)

The Outdoors

After the luncheon, we went down to the pond to check out the ducks, trout, and koi. We also hoped to get a peek at the huge bullfrog and Tripod, the three-legged turtle. Boat rides around the Upper Pond were one of the highlights.

Boat Ride

The Artistry

When we came back into the house, we took out the acrylic paints and lots of paper and started painting freehand. The paintings were wonderful. Before long, all the doors and windows were covered with drying pictures. Justine had one painting that still had globs of wet paint on it when it was time to leave. Michelle was patient with her but finally said it was past time to go. Her painting was very, very wet. She took another piece of paper to blot it. When she peeled up the blotter, it revealed the most gorgeous butterfly. I "Ooh-ed and Aah-ed" over it. I even snapped a picture of her holding it. Out it went to the van, but just before they buckled up, Justine ran back to me and asked if I wanted it. I was touched and thrilled. I framed it right away and put it up on the wall in my living room where it has stayed for years … labelled "Justine's Butterfly." When I opened the frame to clean it recently, I discovered the damp paint had glued the picture to the glass.

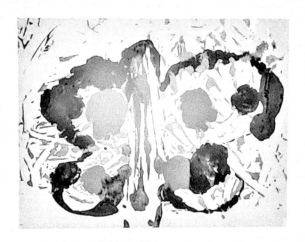

Justine's Butterfly

The Sixth Annual Ladies' Tea Party

Summer, 2001

I had spent the few days before the Sixth Annual Ladies' Tea Party getting ready. Most of my focus was on the food. I had a great time baking up a storm all day Friday giving me time to make the food and the setting look pretty on Saturday morning.

The Menu

Menu	Description
Lemon-Lime Punch	Omit the brandy and rum
Cashew Chicken Loaf	
Sandwiches	Peanut butter, Peanut butter & Honey, Raspberry jelly, Cucumbers, Lettuce,
Condiments	Black olives, Green olives, Pickles, Mustard, Mayo
Fruit Compote	Cantaloupe, Honeydew, Banana, Green & Red grapes, Yogurt
Mini-Muffins	Carrot-Pineapple
Cheese	Cheese Ball & Crackers
Salad	Lettuce, red onion, green pepper, tomato, Water chestnuts,
Lemon Bread	
Petit-Fours	
Tea	Good Earth Original (Herb)

The Attendees

Connie and Michelle arrived with Tavish (her new Westie) and five little girls. Unfortunately, Michelle had to take Justine home because she was suffering from a migraine. Connie and the girls took Tavish (her Westie) and Mickey (my easy-going Rat Terrier) down to the back patio and got them settled in the pen. By that time, I had finally made it to the front door. No one was there! I was scratching my head when they all came back around from below. In came four cheery girls in their Sunday finest: Emma, Chelsea, Kimberly, and Breanna. Kimberly took over for Michelle and made sure Breanna was well taken care of ... minding her manners. Carol came with Stephanie and Brittany. Four adults and six little ladies. We were off and running for the sixth time!

A Very Odd Discovery

Harry had been out looking at antique planes at a nearby airport and made the mistake of coming home a little too early. In order to escape the excitement, he took the dogs for a walk down by the pond. Immediately, four little girls went running down the hill to see him. He beat it back to the house, put the dogs back in the pen, and drove off into the "sunset" pronto. It was pretty funny!

An Olive Tradition

We served the buffet luncheon in the kitchen. On the first pass, the six girls went through one can of large olives. I opened another can, but by then, everyone had their plate filled. After eating, they went out to see the dogs. They found more olives when they returned. Then we had the "Parade of Olive Fingers" as the two youngest (seven and four) demonstrated how olives fit one-to-a-finger. Afterward, we strolled down by the waterfall for a painting experience.

The Last-Annual Painting Party!

Some of the little ladies wanted to paint, others just wanted to explore the waterfall. The painters were so nicely dressed that I grabbed some of Harry's old shirts and passed them around. (He had wanted to toss them, but I knew they'd come in handy!) The youngest girls looked pretty cute in the oversized shirts. I discovered the amount of paint on a paint shirt is inversely proportional to the age of the painter.

This was our third episode with paint. I think I've finally learned not to do it ever again. The birdhouses were painted on the deck, the butterflies were painted on the pool table, and finally I got the location right … this year we painted rocks on sheets and towels in the middle of the road down near the waterfall. A fitting end to painting.

Playing Near The Waterfall

We all returned to enjoy some sweet tea and Petit Fours. The Petit Fours were pretty, and tasty, but didn't seem to go over as well as tea cookies.

The Hunt for Black Olives

After everyone left, I had to hunt for some things in the refrigerator. I had some leftover olive juice to pour over the remaining olives, but I couldn't find the remains of the second can of olives. I just couldn't figure out where Carol or Connie had put them. I looked twice on each shelf, in the door, and in the crispers. I simply couldn't find them. I looked three times on the condiment shelf. Finally, I called Carol and we solved the mystery. THE GIRLS ATE TWO WHOLE CANS OF LARGE OLIVES … TWO!!!

The Seventh Annual Ladies' Tea Party

August 24, 2002

Preparations for a Ladies' Tea Party start weeks, sometimes months, in advance.

Behind the Scenes ... "No Rush"

Monday night, almost three weeks before the Tea Party, my mixer died. It was a freak accident. The pin holding everything together sheared off while I was whipping two eggs ... a crucial component in peppermint cookies. I took the mixer in for repairs the following day. They said it would be a simple problem to fix ... and I might have it back in two or three days. "No problem," I said, "No rush!"

On Thursday, I called to check on the status. There was a little problem: The regular repairman had heart trouble and was scheduled for open-heart surgery the following Tuesday. They acknowledged my mixer wasn't fixed, but they were interviewing people to help out. "No problem," I said, "No rush!" When I got off the phone, I made bread by hand ... which included all the gooey-sticky stuff that goes with mixing bread by hand. I missed my mixer.

The following week, I was at the beach and received two phone messages on my recorder: (1) my machine was irreparably damaged, and (2) please call. On Thursday, I called to check on the status of the machine. They hadn't done anything because blah, blah, blah and did I want to repair it for a lot of money, or just buy a new one for a lot more money? "Let's repair it," I said, "and can I have it back by Wednesday, August 21?" I was beginning to worry when their response was, "We'll try."

On Tuesday, I called again. They were trying to get it done by Wednesday or Thursday. The new man, Steve, said he'd call me for sure on Wednesday to let me know how things were progressing. Wednesday came and went, but at 2:00 p.m., Thursday, Steve called and announced my mixer was repaired. I picked it up that afternoon.

My Plans ... Harry's Plans

Being without my mixer forced me to sit in front of the computer and organize the Tea Party. It didn't take long before everything came together. Here's what I had planned.

Menu	
Lemon-Lime Punch	Lemon, Lime, Carbonated Sprite Punch Bowl - Ice Blocks with pansies
Cashew Chicken Loaf	Could have used a single batch instead of double
Vegetable Potato Salad	Could have used a single batch instead of double
Fruit Salad	Annette – Melon Balls
Sandwiches	2 Valtrompia loaves of bread Peanut Butter, Apricot-Pineapple Jelly, Cucumbers (3)
Condiments	Black olives and Green olives Kalamata Olives (didn't need) Dill pickles, Mustard, Mayo
Tea	Good Earth Original (Herbal Tea) – 11 tea bags
Bird's Nests	Made from Shredded Wheat and Marshmallow Creme, these made great place decorations
Dessert	Connie – Berry-Pudding-Cake Melange
Orange wafers	(Thin and pretty … but not a big hit)
Chocolate Cottage Cookies	Went over well (but they were a little dry)

Shopping List	
5 cups Chicken	Green Olives
1 cup cashews	Black Olives
1 cup Half & Half	8 medium potatoes
3 packages cream cheese	Green Giant Corn
Good Earth Tea	Celery
Limeade – 12 oz (2)	Green Pepper
Lemonade 12 oz (2)	Sweet onion
Lime Garnish	Beans for eyes
Peanut Butter	Marshmallows
Jam	Shredded Wheat
Cucumber (2)	Mints
Green Lettuce	Flour
Milk	Sugar
Radishes	Chocolate Raisins

Set Out
Tables
Centerpieces
Napkins
Silverware
Tables/Chairs/Cloths
S&P Shakers
Glasses, punch bowl
Cucumbers/Paprika
Bread Platter
Cookie Platters
Condiments and juice containers

Harry, on the other hand, had planned to go away on a golfing weekend.

Poof!

Thursday night was dedicated to purchasing the groceries. Friday was dedicated to baking … starting with bread at 10:00 a.m. I put all the ingredients in the bowl and turned my newly-repaired mixer on very, very low … "Poof!" Flour left the machine traveling Instantaneously and simultaneously north, east, south, and west … all over the baking area. My ten-speed mixer now had only two speeds: fast and faster! Although this was a good thing for mixing eggs, it was decidedly difficult for adding all the dry ingredients I had planned to use that day. Fortunately, I had plenty of towels. A fresh towel served as a

mixer cover for each batch of "whatever" including: Orange
Cookies, Chocolate Cookies, and two batches of bread.

Poof!

I saw Harry off about noon, then baked, chopped, sliced, and
diced my way through the day, into the evening, and finally
into the wee hours of the morning. The bird and the dogs tried
to keep pace but all three crashed by midnight as I was getting my third wind. Before I went to bed, I had several plates
of cookies, several bags of bread, a large bowl of potato salad,
and a Cashew Chicken Loaf squeezed into the refrigerator like
the Pillsbury Dough Boy stuffed into a bumper car.

The Morning Of

On Saturday, with little else to do except make sure the house was ready for company, I sat down to say my morning prayers. There were several things I could have done, like fix centerpieces, make sure all the napkins were pre-folded, or set the tables, but praying seemed the more important and prudent course of action. By 12:30 p.m., everything was ready except the centerpieces, napkins, and tablecloths (they never quite made it to the top of the list). I showered and got ready for company, and sure enough about 12:50 p.m., people started arriving.

The Arrival

Carol came first with Stephanie and Brittany. In their hands were bouquets of roses and mums … unexpected centerpieces for the tables! Check!

Next came another Carol and her daughter, Acacia. Acacia's hair was braided around her head like a crown, with delicate little rosebuds gracing the wreath. She was wearing a dress from the previous year's Christmas pageant. Her doll, Rosie, had a matching dress. Without the proper furniture for Rosie, we found an emergency perch for her on the little counter at the top of the stairs. It could have been tragic if she had needed acrobatic skills, but no mishaps occurred.

Almost immediately, Annette followed with her daughters: Jasmine, Amber, and Christina … all in sun bonnets!

Then came Maggie and her daughter, Myrtice.

Connie came in with yet another beautiful bouquet of roses! Michelle brought Justine, Chelsea, Kimberly, and Breanna, who suddenly appeared in front of me looking up with the biggest, most expectant eyes and a smile to match. (She was quite eager to experience this year's Tea Party. She was first in line for food during the luncheon and first to pour tea at the table during dessert.)

After introductions, Carol and the girls took the centerpieces and the tablecloths out to the backyard and dressed the tables. Carol and Acacia volunteered to take the napkins and silverware out to the tables. And just like that, all my concerns about centerpieces, napkins, and tablecloths disappeared. Check, check and check!

Very Chic

Unbeknownst to me, Carol and Acacia discovered the napkins were not all folded identically. Carol said they needed to all be folded alike, but Acacia said they were fine. Carol wasn't convinced. They studied how one of the napkins was folded. After a little squinting, they folded all the other napkins to match. All the places look very chic indeed with napkins alternating white and mauve around all the tables.

The Punch

The Lemon-Lime Punch was an experiment to see if I could make a nice punch using the punchbowl and ice blocks. The flowers in the ice blocks were not visible, but the floating sliced limes looked very appealing. The first batch of punch was made according to a recipe, using Sprite as the liquid. After noticing how much "energy" it gave the girls and realizing the cans of juice were sweet enough, we opted to make the second batch of punch according to the label ... with water ... it turned out to be a very good idea! I had misjudged the number of glasses needed for the day. Stephanie, a willing partner, dried the punch glasses as fast as I could turn them out.

Solo Woke Up

After a bit of visiting and sipping, some of the girls decided to go out on the deck to explore. I saw them leave to the left. A few minutes later, they came running back with terrified looks sprinting past the side door and around to the main part of the deck. Sure enough, five seconds later, up came Solo, our 95-pound shaggy Bouvier des Flandres, loping past the first door to see who dared to intrude on our deck. By the time I got outside, Solo had started barking. I had to thank him and assure him the girls were expected. (Solo was probably embarrassed because he had let all these people come onto the property without announcing their arrival.) Once I acknowledged I knew they were there, he ceased barking! Peace.

Solo on Guard Duty

The Place Cards

An important job had yet to be done. Place cards were ready to be set out. Brittany and I dashed out to the tables and arranged the settings by age groups … but not by family. Brittany gave me a shy smile as she put her own place card close to Stephanie and next to others her own age.

The Blessing

A couple of days before the party, I had asked Acacia to lead our blessing on Saturday. She had willingly agreed. After we had our punch and got to know each other a little bit, Acacia led us in a blessing ... for our day, for our friendships, for our food ... and off we went to fill our plates with colorful edibles.

The Peanut Butter

The girls had been looking forward to making their own sandwiches. With bread shaped like daisies and hearts, with cucumbers, mayo, and lettuce, and with peanut butter and apricot-pineapple jam to choose from, each person who wanted a special sandwich began producing her masterpiece. Others could have some of the Cashew-Chicken Loaf.

Breanna was the first to make it through the sandwich line. Out she popped, ready to have some salad and melon balls. She reached up for the veggie-potato salad, took one look at it, and moved over to the melon balls and olives. I was behind her, curling over her head like a six-foot question mark. From my vantage point, I could see a small glob of peanut butter stuck to the front of her cheek. There was absolutely no way I could possibly reach my camera to take a picture. I had to be satisfied with searing it into my memory.

The Butterflies

Given the option of making floral butterflies or making faces with food, Kimberly chose butterflies and went to announce the craft to the other girls. Annette, Michelle, Carol, and I busied ourselves cutting butterfly bases out of card stock. For a while, it seemed we would be the only ones having any craft fun. We were cutting with reckless abandon. Paper scraps were dropping here and there ... holes were poked ... wires were shaped into antennae.

Soon, in came the girls, each with a handful of colorful flowers or leaves (and even dirt)! They began gluing, drawing, and coloring on the butterflies. Everyone was crowded around the rattan glass-topped table, working their hearts out. (The extra mini-mints, in a little candy dish in the center of the table, slowly disappeared.) Acacia and Kimberly, needing a little more room, found just the right place at the covered pool table. Everyone else bumped into each other with amazingly intense focus creating these "living" butterflies. (School teachers must enjoy craft time.)

As we were beginning preparations for taking our tea in the garden, I remember looking up noticing Michelle give the craft table one final wipe: glue, scraps, wires, and flowers had all miraculously disappeared ... the colorful butterflies were all on the coffee table.

The Helper

Jasmine asked to help and I accepted. She had her hand in everything ... from doing the math to determine how many tea bags we should use ... to vigorously stirring the tea bags ... to carrying platters. I put her in charge of taking out the platters of cookies when we were about to serve the tea. She returned with one of the platters untouched saying we had enough cookies out there and didn't need that platter. Will wonders never cease?

After tea, everyone including Brittany raced down to the pen to see Mickey. Jasmine, on the other hand, came over to the tables with the adults and thanked us all for the Tea Party!

Before they went home, all the girls had their pictures taken with their butterflies, and then they were off. I began looking forward to the next year. New plans to make, new recipes to find.

Was Mickey Traumatized?

The jury was out on this question.

Mickey, our little rat terrier, is used to a quiet life. Anytime something unexpected happens, he runs to Harry or me and stands between our legs looking out at the scary thing. It's his safe spot. Naturally, I failed to take this into account as the Tea Party progressed. In fact, I totally spaced out and left the poor little guy to fend for himself. Though I didn't witness it, I later heard he was invited to jump up into Justine's arms … and did it! Thank goodness she caught him! As more and more girls wanted to fuss over him, he sought shelter between Amber's ankles. Myrtice and Acacia realized what was happening. Myrtice scooped him up and held him securely before he was totally overwhelmed by this bevy of little beauties.

That evening, I fed the dogs. Mickey didn't eat his dinner. The poor little guy's routine had been thoroughly upset. When I sat down to rest, he crashed in my lap as if he'd never wake up again. The next morning, I fed him breakfast in the pen, as usual. When I got home from church, he still hadn't eaten much. I was beginning to think he was totally traumatized.

Harry came home a couple of hours later and listened to my concerns. I told him about the party and how the girls had gone down to the pond. When I told him I had seen the girls leaning into the fish food barrel, Harry discovered the reason behind Mickey's dilemma ... he was stuffed. Mickey had always enjoyed fish food more than kibble. So much for being traumatized!

Was Mickey Traumatized?

Eighth Annual Ladies' Tea Party

August, 2003

B y the time, the Eighth Annual Ladies' Tea Party, came around, the original girls had grown up and new little girls had been added. We had fewer attendees than ever before: three women (Carol, Janet and myself), two young ladies (Stephanie and Brittany) and a four-year-old (Janet's daughter Jenae). The only word that seemed to summarize this Tea Party was "YIKES!"

A Special Day for Baking

The day before a Tea Party was always hectic in a structured way ... it was my special day for baking. I started by baking bread ... two free-form loaves and three designer loaves in the familiar heart, star, and flower shapes. I had to go to the store for some last-minute necessities. When I came back, I popped two different quiches in the oven (recipes to follow). After the luncheon quiches were half-finished baking, I discovered the melted butter still in the microwave. Oops! There was no way to mix it in with the cooked ingredients, but I did manage to drizzle a couple of tablespoons over the top. That was the best I could do. With the quiche on its way, I made some tiny honey-wheat muffins and mixed up a sugar-free cream cheese topping. My last duty was to chop up some vegetables for a colorful salad. The day was finished, and so was I!

The Gift

In past years, I'd been rushing around at the last minute trying to do extra little things that weren't part of the plan. For this party, however, everything was ready just as my guests drove up. Carol, Brittany, and Stephanie came first. Janet was just arriving. If I had left well-enough alone, I could have greeted everyone with a warm, calm smile. However, just at the last minute, I thought it would be ever-so-helpful if I pulled the strawberries out of the freezer. Just as Janet and Jenae came in, I bumped the refrigerator shelf, and down fell a box of strawberries. The container didn't break, and nothing was damaged, but little red strawberry droplets scattered all over a ten-square-foot area of the tiled kitchen floor. (I don't know how the droplets escaped the container without the strawberries following, but that's exactly what happened.) I gulped, grabbed for a paper towel, wiped up the mess, and greeted everyone, faking calmness. Jenae gave me a little gift bag containing among other things, some Sleepytime Tea. I didn't realize how much I would need it before the day was done!

Feeding Donald

Our first task was to feed Donald …

A few years earlier, at the end of the school year, a kindergarten teacher at the school where I was tutoring math asked if anyone wanted to have one or more little ducklings. I was thrilled! I took my four little treasures home (three variegated ducklings and one slightly larger light-colored duckling). I put them in the pond with high hopes of raising them forever. They found a nice place to hide from predators and started foraging for food. The next day, there were only three ducklings. I felt bad, and tried to rationalize, thinking "Survival of the fittest." I couldn't do anything to protect them because I couldn't get anywhere near them. They scurried away from me and found hiding places wherever they could. The next day, there were only two. My heartstrings were plucked again. The following day, I was hoping to find the two ducklings, but there were none! I was so disheartened. I walked along the bank of the Lower Pond looking and looking, but there was no one there. I was downcast as I trudged back toward the house. And then I heard a faint little quack. I couldn't imagine where it had come from. I could see the bank four feet below me, clearly. No one was there. But I heard it again. I quacked back. And again, I heard my little phantom. Finally, I curled myself over the outlet and peered into the abyss. The outlet feeds into an eighteen-inch metal culvert, which had been installed at a 45-degree angle. Water gushes out of the pond through that culvert. And there, sitting on the corrugated tube was the stout little duckling with water flowing all around him. I feared for his safety. Any minute he was likely to be swept away by the force of the water. In order to get back into the pond he'd have to make an extraordinary leap upward. There was just no way he could do that. I ran around, like another fowl with her head cut off, looking for a stick or some other tool to use to scoop up my little duckling before his fate was sealed. I ran fifty feet to the slash pile and found something that might work. I ran back as fast as I could to save my little duckling. When I got back to the culvert, I looked over the edge and saw it was empty. I was devastated. I had lost the last of the ducklings. Dejected, I stood up and started to take the stick back to the slash pile when I heard, "Quack … quack!" There he was, paddling along in the middle of the pond. In that moment, I realized Donald, my little duckling, was a survivor!

Donald was a sweet little duck … well, not so little. As he grew, so did his proportions. There was no hiding it … Donald was bottom-heavy! In addition, he wasn't much of a flyer, which meant he stayed at Two Ponds for his whole life. Big domestic ducks like Donald can live for up to ten years …quite a little less when there are predators around. Donald lived a full and happy four years.

Donald was a sociable duck. He would try to engage the mallards when they would fly in for a few days. They were a little nasty to him, perhaps because he looked different. Domestic ducks are from the Mallard family. You'd think they'd be best buddies. Go figure. He enjoyed all four ponds: we, of course, had two ponds, and our neighbors, Maurice and Dorothy, had the other two ponds. Our ponds offered a better chance at hiding from predators, so he stayed around a lot. But when I was off tutoring, he'd go up and visit Maurice and Dorothy.

Maurice taught Donald how to fly … someone had to. Morry was mowing the lawn one day like he was on a mission. Donald was on the dike as Morry was fast approaching. When that noisy lawn-mower got close enough, Donald jumped into the air and flew on a downward trajectory into the next lower pond. With all that weight behind him, it was a pretty fair chore to fly in anything but a downward trajectory, but he learned quickly. Once he experienced flight, he practiced until he could fly from one pond up to the next.

We had planted hundreds of Donaldson Rainbow trout that year. Consequently, we always had plenty of fish food available. Donald kept his "trim" figure by horsing down fish food whenever he could. Donald never missed a good fish feed.

Donald, The Bottom-Heavy Duck

... and so ... all the Tea Party ladies went along the road to the Upper Pond to feed Donald. Jenae got there first. I showed her how to throw one spoonful of fish food at a time and get it far enough out in the pond … the fish were hesitant to approach the bank. Then it became a game to see if we could get the food to the fish before Donald and the rest of the mallards got to it. It was great fun, and it burned off a little energy from those who had too much to start out with.

The ducks were happy to see us. Brittany sat on the bench concentrating intently on the ducks. Donald came up and "talked" with us. It was fun to watch Brittany put fish food on the toe of her tennis shoe and wait for Donald to edge forward and nibble it. It made her giggle!

After a bit, we encouraged the ducks to fly off the edge of the waterfall, down to the Lower Pond, and compete with the older fish in that pond for their lunch. Donald got a little more than his fair share … as usual.

Banana-Strawberry Smoothie

On the way back to the house, Brittany and Jenae checked out the dogs. Brittany is always very good with Mickey. Once we got upstairs, it was time for a Banana-Strawberry Smoothie made with buttermilk. Anyone who was over four years old had a crystal goblet … Jenae was excited about using a little crystal ice cream dish … it looked like a miniature goblet. But first, I gave her a little history about the china and the crystal … about how my grandmother had once owned the dishes and crystal and had given lovely parties many years ago. Always in the past, that had produced a little moment of silence and awe from the girls, but this year … YIKES! I found myself holding onto the little goblet, not daring to let go. I told her we could only use the goblets over the carpet … not over the tile floor.

(All those years I'd been chuckling at my girlfriends who were quaking at the thought of crystal and china crashing onto the tile floor. Now it was my turn to panic.)

Since we were going to have our Smoothies in the living room, I brought Boris and his cage in from the Sunporch. It was just too much for Jenae. She wanted to see him so badly she opted to abandon her Smoothie for a while. I was amused to see her pick it up and set it down about six times over the course of twenty to thirty minutes before she ever actually took a sip.

An Unusual Sandwich

Jenae was pretty anxious to get on with the luncheon. Brittany had requested we make our own sandwiches again this year, so we all paraded into the kitchen to begin our assemblage. I had set out the customary peanut butter, but no jam nor honey since Jenae is "allergic" to sugar. I also had set out ingredients necessary to build a fine cucumber sandwich … just in case any of us would like something a little lighter than peanut butter. There was one little butter spreader with a red handle and several larger knives to use. Jenae immediately grabbed the red handle proclaiming, "I want this one!" She selected a slice of bread shaped like a heart and hacked off more than one tablespoon of butter! I couldn't believe my eyes. It was almost too much for the knife. She stuck it on the bread. I wondered how the peanut butter was going to fit in her sandwich. Just then, she took another slice of bread and pressed it up against the monstrous pat of butter. She was finished. She was having a Butter Sandwich … no need for peanut butter when you have the real thing! And so we continued.

Brittany Assisted with Creating a Recipe

Brittany and I collaborated on what to put in the salad, wanting it to be tasty and colorful. We had decided on cubed white potatoes, red and yellow peppers, diced white onion, purple grapes, red lettuce, green peas and broccoli, and pecan halves. It looked and tasted great!

The Lucky Place

After dishing up our plates, we went outside to the picnic table where pink napkins, a white tablecloth with purple accents, and green plants awaited. I was the last one out and was tickled to find Jenae dancing around excitedly. She was in seventh heaven because she was sitting in "The Lucky Place." Enclosed in her napkin, she had found some bubbles and a wand. She told me over and over how lucky she was to have gotten "The Lucky Place." Janet told me Jenae would be talking about "The Lucky Place" for weeks … and without a doubt, in a couple of months, there'd be another reference to "The Lucky Place!"

An Unexpected Pause in the Festivities

We ate our lunch near the Maid's Garden, overlooking the Lower Pond. After lunch, it looked as though Janet was going to have to go home to take care of Julie, Jenae's younger sister. Janet's husband, John, was taking some classes, and Julie, who had been sleeping when it was time to leave to go to the party, was his little charge. But when it was time for him to go to class, Julie became Janet's little charge. Julie was welcome, and it didn't take too much effort to convince Janet to go get her. Stephanie went with her. While they were gone, Carol, Brittany, and I were entertained by Jenae blowing bubbles. She must have used the bubble wand at least a dozen times without hardly making a dent in the mixture. Then, all of a sudden, we noticed it was empty. (I wondered where it went!)

Brewing the Tea

Brewing the tea is a complicated process. I asked Jenae to help me select the bags. She was up for it. It's also "quite important" to get just the right amount of water in the pitcher. She sat on the counter while we were waiting for Janet and Stephanie to return. I opened the bags, plopped them in a glass pitcher, and pointed to an imaginary line about halfway up the pitcher. Jenae's job was to turn the handle on the boiling-water spigot and keep it turned until the water got up to my finger. Because the handle is hard to turn and she was leaning awkwardly to the left, she needed to concentrate on her job. As the water approached the imaginary line, I inched my finger slowly up the side of the pitcher. She continued to concentrate, I continued to inch. I was having fun, but it was also looking as if I'd never be able to cool it down in time, so we had to stop at the three-quarter mark to let the tea steep.

Beads

It was only fifteen minutes before Janet, Stephanie, and Julie returned. It was time to do a craft. We sat down to make some beaded bracelets, anklets, and necklaces. Janet had brought a huge collection of beads. All we had to do was supply the imagination. Jenae set about creating a very colorful necklace only to get distracted. Janet made a bracelet and an anklet for a friend. Brittany made a pretty teal bracelet to match her top. Stephanie made a necklace with a cross for me. I made a little pink and purple necklace for my niece. When we were all finished, it was time for a little photo op. Jenae decided she didn't like her bead project at all and saw no need to get in the picture ... but the rest of us smiled and posed.

"I Want Some Tea"

More than anything, Jenae wanted to have some tea. The time had come. I served the tea in the living room and positioned Jenae in a central position. I didn't realize how anxious I was becoming, until that wriggly four-year-old had to scooch past the maximum number of people to get to freedom. I relocated her to an end spot. I hope I've learned my lesson.

I brought out the Honey-Wheat muffins. The Buttermilk Cream Cheese topping had been piped on with a cake decorator. They were pretty, but one of us didn't care for the taste. Guess which one! Before long, I had two toppings in my hand. They had been peeled-off and handed to me by Jenae. It looked as if I was going to get more. She pulled her hands back and Carol jumped: It seemed like there were twenty-five sticky fingers on that one little girl, but I'm pretty sure she only had the usual ten.

"Be careful, that's Uncle Harry's special chair ... Let's go wash our hands," I invited. We went into the bathroom. I hoisted her up to the sink, helping her reach the water ... but she wouldn't have anything to do with the soap. The more I insisted, the more she unhoisted herself until she finally yelled, "Ouch!" Her little tummy was getting pinched against the counter. I lost the soap contest. (Point: Jenae) After we finished, I got out a little stool in case we had to wash up again. Freshly washed, we returned to the party.

Can We Say "No?"

I often find it difficult to say "no," so I'm always looking for creative ways to get around it. This time, with Harry not in attendance, and with an overly-inquisitive Jenae being unfamiliar with him, anything I wanted to be "off limits" automatically became Harry's. On the way back to the living room we had a little back-and-forth repartee: she wanted to play the piano, but it was Uncle Harry's piano. She still wanted to play the piano, but sadly, it was still Uncle Harry's piano. (Point: Kathy)

Another time, when we were all in the living room, Jenae and I had a little discussion about the dogs:

"Let's go see the dogs."

"The dogs are taking a nap."

"Where?"

"Downstairs."

"Where?"

"Downstairs."

"But where ... where is Mickey?"

"Mickey is in his pen staying warm."

"And where is Solo?"

"Solo is in his bed."

"Where?"

"In the bedroom." (I couldn't hold out any longer.)

"Can I go see him."

"He's in Uncle Harry's bedroom." (I recovered.)

"Can I go in Uncle Harry's bedroom."

"Only Uncle Harry goes in his bedroom."

(Discussion over. Point: Kathy)

"I Have to Go Poop."

Everyone was deep in conversation about school and other things. Suddenly, I saw Jenae leave the room, and heard her say, "I have to go poop." She had already hiked her dress way up to her waist, exposing her bright purple panties, and was marching quickly and determinedly to the bathroom.

"Need any help?" I hollered.

"Yeah," she said. And off I went. She was doubled over on the pot by the time I got there.

I flicked on the lights. "Want some light?" I asked.

"No," she blurted out.

I flicked off the lights. There we were, two buddies ... together ... accomplishing our task. She casually confided, "I always have to go poop after I eat muffins."

Just as casually, I replied, "Yeah, me too."

Finally (and quickly, I might add) the deed was done. Now it was my turn to go to work. I don't remember if I gave any instructions, but almost instantly she was upside-down (or should I say backside-up). One wipe was successfully accomplished. "I always wipe twice," I said hurriedly, fearing one wipe wouldn't do the trick. Patiently, she waited staring at the floor which was a mere two inches from her nose. I wiped; she pulled up; I flushed, and she started to leave.

"Hey, Hey, Hey!" I jumped. "Not so fast. We have to wash our hands!"

Up she went on the stool. I handed her a bar of soap, saying, "I always use soap when I go poop."

She reached for the soap, replying sweetly, "So do I." (Point: Kathy)

Everyone was laughing up a storm when we returned. They gathered up their things to leave. Jenae, half-bolting out the door, paused in mid-step, looked back, raised her hand and yelled, "Thanks for the Tea Party, Kath!" … and out she went.

Running Around Chasing Holly

Everyone was packed in the car and just about to leave when Harry came home with Holly, our new little Schipperke puppy. Brittany, who visited us often throughout the year, got to know our dogs quite well. She loved Holly, and really wanted to see her before they left. I brought our little black furball to the front yard where they were all waiting. In a brave but possibly fool-hardy gesture, I let her off the leash. She discovered Jenae and couldn't get enough of her. The feeling was mutual. She raced around the yard like greased lightning with Jenae chasing her. It was obvious we should have done this much earlier. They were made for each other. But eventually, Holly got tired of playing "Catch Me If You Can" and decided to go exploring. She headed toward the cul-de-sac on a fast trot. I took a deep breath and did my best low-pitched imitation of Harry. "Holly ... No!" She stopped and looked. "Holly ... Sit!" She thought about it and then sat. Jenae patiently waited while I walked up to Holly and slipped the lead over her head. We had one false start but a second "Sit!" did the trick.

Holly was back under control ... and the Eighth Annual Ladies' Tea Party came to a satisfactory conclusion.

Although I had made copious note, the write-up wasn't completely finished until the day before the Ninth Annual Ladies' Tea Party ... after a full year of rest!

The Recipes

Quiche #1 For the 8th Annual Ladies' Tea Party
1 10-oz. pkg frozen vegetables, cooked and drained
1 cup dairy sour cream
1 cup creamed cottage cheese
½ cup baking mix
¼ cup margarine or butter, melted
2 eggs
1 tomato, peeled, thinly sliced
¼ cup grated Parmesan Cheese
Heat oven to 350 degrees. Grease pie plate: 9-by-1¼ inches. Spread vegetables in plate. Beat sour cream, cottage cheese, baking mix, margarine and eggs until smooth (15 seconds in blender or 1 minute with hand beater). Pour into plate. Arrange tomato slices on top. Sprinkle with Parmesan cheese. Bake until knife inserted in center comes out clean: about 30 minutes. Cool 5 minutes. Makes 6 – 8 servings

Quiche #2 For the 8th Annual Ladies' Tea Party

½ pound cubed ham
1 pkg frozen spinach
½ cup chopped white onion
1 cup Swiss Cheese (about 4 oz.)
2 cups milk
1 cup baking mix
4 eggs
¼ teaspoon salt
1 dash, pepper
1 tbsp Worchestershire Sauce

Heat oven to 400 degrees. Grease a 13x9x2 glass pan. Combine ham, spinach and onion in large bowl. Using a blender, beat remaining ingredients until smooth (15 seconds). Pour into bowl and stir until thoroughly mixed. Pour into pan. Bake until knife inserted in center comes out clean, 40-45 minutes. Cool 5 minutes. Makes twelve 3"x3" servings.

Baking Mix

2 cups all-purpose flour
½ teaspoon salt
½ cup shortening
4 teaspoons baking powder
¼ teaspoon baking soda
2 teaspoons sugar (optional)

The Ninth Annual Ladies' Tea Party

August 28, 2004

With eight Tea Parties under my belt, I decided to add more to my schedule. I attended a baby shower next door. I allotted 10:30 a.m. through noon for my baby shower attendance. Even though I had to leave before the shower was over, I had a great time and found it to be a very pleasant way of relaxing before everyone came.

Inviting Kiersten

Kiersten (seven) is a friend of Jenae (five). Inviting Kiersten was an event in itself. I'm glad I didn't miss it! I had met her once when she was playing with Jenae, but doubted if she remembered me. I called her to see if she'd like to come to the Tea Party. After introducing myself to Karen, her mother, I soon found myself talking with Kiersten.

Nine Feet Tall

"How are you?" she chirped. She's a chirper! A breathy one, at that.

"I'm fine; how are you?"

"I'm fine, too. Do you still have the fish?" And off our conversation went in the direction of the ponds.

"How deep is your pond?" She asked.

"Well, how tall is your Daddy?" I countered.

"Oh, he's about nine feet."

"Oh, my pond is a little bit deeper than that."

"Just a minute," she faltered. "I'll check and see how tall my Daddy is." ("How tall is Daddy?" she asked her mother.) … finally, "He's six feet four inches."

"Oh … my pond is way deeper than that."

Old is Relative

(During a brief lull, I turned on my recorder … I didn't want to miss a single word!)

Unexpectedly, she said, "Oh … I'm watching 'Parent Trap III'."

Now I was really excited, "Oh, that's a good movie. I saw 'Parent Trap I'."

"Yes, that's really old." (At that point I was extremely impressed she even knew about "Parent Trap I." I was also impressed that she appreciated it was really old, since it came out in 1961, more than forty years earlier!) But she burst my bubble by declaring "It came out when I was two." (I guess old is relative.)

After a little more conversation, I invited her to the Tea Party. She made sure it was okay with her Mother, and then surprised me by asking if she should bring anything.

We talked some more about what she might expect at a Tea Party, and since Karen was under the weather, I suggested she take very really good care of her Mommy.

"I cleaned my room, which she wanted me to, and I fixed my bed, which she wanted me to," she assured me.

Allergies

I had to make sure she didn't have any major dislikes in the way of food. I asked if there was anything she was allergic to.

"I'm allergic to Windex ... and ... I'm allergic to ... and also pollen ... well ... maybe not pollen ... but I'm allergic to Windex. I sneeze when I'm around Windex." After a bit I was able to finally discover she had no food allergies.

Smelly Nails and a Sleepover

I asked her what she was going to wear. She said she had a beautiful green silk dress, but when confronted with the possibility of playing with dogs, she also mentioned she had a sunflower dress, which was red and had daisies on it. I tried to imagine the combination of red and daisies, which would make a person think of the dress as a sunflower dress, to no avail.

"Do you think I should paint my nails? ... because I have some nail polish, and it smells."

"Oh! You should do that today so it won't smell tomorrow!"

"Why?" She sounded hurt. (I'm so out of touch.)

"What kind is it?" I queried, trying hard to get back on board.

"It's pink, and it smells like strawberry."

"Oh, that would be just perfect because we're going to have strawberries and lemonade."

"What are you wearing?" She picked up the previous conversation without breaking stride.

(Oops, I didn't have a clue how to answer that!) "I'm wearing a dress, or if I don't have a dress, I have a lovely blue skirt I can wear."

"What are you doing?"

"I'm getting ready for the Tea Party, making bread so we can have sandwiches with bread shaped like little flowers."

"Ohhh!"

She asked if her sister could come, but I let her know this was special, just for her. She mentioned her sister had gone on a sleepover. I asked if she'd ever gone on a sleepover. Of course, the answer had to be yes because she and Jenae were such good friends.

"Once, I had a sleepover with Jenae, and she kept me up all night."

"How did she do that?"

"Well … she said 'Kiersten, I need to go to the bathroom.' and … 'Kiersten, I'm thirsty.' and … 'Kiersten, I'm hot.'"

Foolishly, I thought she was staying over at Jenae's, so I asked, "Why did she say that?"

"Well, I had to bring her a glass of water, and she needed me to show her where the bathroom was because she couldn't find it in the dark. Have you seen Janet's new room?"

"No, but I'm looking forward to it!"

"It has a bunch of windows. There are windows on the side wall."

And so on.

One O'Clock

Finally, we closed by confirming the start time of the Tea Party as one o'clock. She said, "One o'clock … I'd better write it down. I'll write 1:00 or one o'clock. All right. One second, I have to do something. (Pause) You see, I was holding it with my writing hand, and I had to switch ears. (Pause) One … O' … Clock. (Pause) I write bad." With that, she had an incoming call so we cut the conversation "short."

The Arrivals

Carol, Stephanie (sixteen) and Brittany (thirteen) arrived first. Carol looked at her copy of the write-up from the previous year and did a nice reading of "I Have to Go Poop." I read "The Lucky Place." It put us all in a great mood for the event.

Connie came next with Kimberly (nine) and Breanna (seven). The start of school was just around the corner. We talked about who was going where and when school starts. After a bit, we had some refreshments. While we were pouring, Janet drove up with Julie (three), Jenae (five), and Kiersten (seven). All at once, there was more commotion than I could handle. But Kimberly put spray-cheese on the crackers, and all the drinks were eventually poured and served. We did a little more visiting to get ourselves settled. Even with Diet Snapple (i.e., no sugar), it wasn't too long before some of us were antsy to go for a walk.

Feeding Fowl; Flinging Food

When the older guests got to the Upper Pond, Jenae was already busy telling Kiersten, Breanna, and Kimberly how to stand to feed the fish. She planted her body at a 90-degree to the pond indicating how to do the follow-through. I had to hurry a little to get down there to see how much fish food was in the bucket. The fish and ducks combined don't eat more than about three scoops. The girls were very patient and seemed to understand how to ration the food to avoid running out. Everyone seemed ready to share. They were thrilled when they could rile up the young trout and get the water boiling with a feeding frenzy.

A Slip and Clean Shoes

Breanna was the bravest of them all. She was wearing tennis shoes and appeared sure-footed. She climbed out on a rock just above the waterfall and posed for a picture ... and another ... and another. There's something about being seven. After she left the rock, another little person arrived, less sure-footed than Breanna, but if you let one do it, how can you say "No" to three others. I was trapped, so the camera kept clicking. I warned them some of the rocks were loose. I failed to mention the loose ones were way behind them. It worked, though, because everyone became ultra-cautious. So far, so good.

Breanna was working her way down to the Lower Pond ... on the river rock. All of a sudden, we heard the nasty sound of something splashing into the water. It was Breanna ... she had tumbled. There she was in a long dress, tennis shoes, and white socks. When all was said and done, her dress was still dry, but her shoes and socks were soaked. Taking this as a cue, we abandoned the fish and ducks and went back up to the house to have our luncheon, with a quick stop to visit the dogs and get replacement shoes and socks for Breanna … mine … size nine … but they stayed on her feet!

A Bug on the Skirt Ends in a Catastrophe

On the way back up to the house, one of the girls noticed I had a caterpillar on my skirt. Connie remarked we were in for a cold, hard winter because it was a very fuzzy caterpillar. The girls seemed totally fascinated. By the time we got to the front door, they were looking for a jar so they could put the caterpillar safely inside with some leaves. Not wanting to cut off its air supply, I looked in my cupboard for a nice wine glass … oops … no, not that one … I found a wine glass I'd be willing to lose. The Grand Canyon glass seemed to be a natural. With a flourish about how nice it was with the gold trim, I set them up with a new roofless home for their pet. Kiersten was semi-distraught the caterpillar might crawl out but seemed to be able to live with it.

I went over to the tables with some last-minute things to do. Half the people were at the tables, the other half were still at the front door, when I heard something that sounded like a crystal chandelier crashing to the ground. I decided to ignore it … maybe it would go away. A few seconds later, Kiersten rushed over, out-of-breath (she talks fast, anyway) and told me about the caterpillar which was "in the glass … with the leaves

… on the porch … by the plants …" There were perhaps a half-dozen more prepositional phrases before she took a breath. She finally finished with, "Well … it break-ded!" Trying hard not to smile, I asked a clarifying question. Sure enough, she repeated the whole litany ending with, "… it break-ded!" Janet took control of the whole situation … a little dust-buster action fixed everything. (I was happy Breanna was wearing shoes, not just toughing it with socks!) I lost track of the caterpillar and never saw it again.

Putting Together the Plates

The sandwiches were a little plainer this year, but the salads were colorful: Connie brought a vegetable salad; Carol brought a fruit salad. Outside went the salads. The whole process of fixing plates goes so fast we almost forgot to dish up the quiche. Carol and Connie were watching their little charges so intently they totally missed getting some quiche and had to run back in before we started eating. Why was quiche always a stumbling block?

A Blessing Together

Before we started, I invited someone to volunteer to say a prayer. Much to my surprise and pleasure, Kiersten spoke up. I was amazed. I announced Kiersten was going to lead us in a prayer, but the whole idea of leading anything threw her for a loop. She backed out. I encouraged her to just say it out loud, instead of leading us, but she was still too shy. After the third attempt to encourage her, she was gone for good. Stephanie jumped in and saved the day.

Yellow Jackets in the Sun

No sooner had we started eating than we were visited by a bevy of yellow jackets. We were all sitting in the sun, waving our hands, and hoping they'd go away. There's an island of vegetation in the middle of the lawn in the backyard. I pondered ... perhaps next year, we could have the party on the far side of the island for a little more shade, if we could have it outside at all. Maybe a yellow-jacket trap would be in order, too.

Jane of the Jungle

After finishing their meals, the four youngest were ready to move, but the rest of us were ready to stay. They asked if they could go down to see the dogs. With an affirmative response and a warning not to open the cage or Holly would run away, they were off. One of the hits was the black rope at the corner of the house. I had used it to stabilize a hammock in the past and never took it down. You can run down the hill, grab the rope, and get airborne, and if you are ancient and have a memory or an imagination, you can be Jane of the Jungle! Who knew it would end up being a thing? Breanna took up residence on the rope and did a little swinging around the corner. It was nice because it was one way to keep an eye on them.

A Parade of Dogs

When the older ladies finally finished lunch, one of the girls made a request to take the dogs for a walk. I had three dogs: Solo (Bouvier des Flandres), Holly Bear (Schipperke), and

Mickey (Rat Terrier). It was very funny because three girls were talking at the same time.

Kiersten said, "I want the big black dog!"

Breanna said, "I want the little black dog!"

Jenae said, "I want Mickey!"

I got some leashes from the garage.

As the girls followed me in, Kiersten said, "I want the big black dog!"

Breanna said, "I want the little black dog!"

Jenae said, "I want Mickey!"

They were constant and consistent, certain if they didn't keep telling me, they wouldn't get the one they wanted. Sometimes I heard big black dog, Mickey, little black dog, other times I heard big black ... LITTLE black ... I want Mickey. But always they continued nonstop. So, being a big fan of asking clarifying questions when none are needed, I stepped in ...

"Kiersten, do you want the big black dog?"

"Yes!"

"I want the little black dog," Breanna interjected.

"Breanna, do you want the little black dog?"

"Yes!"

"And Jenae, do you want Mickey?"

"Yes!"

"Okay then, I'll leash them up."

But off they prattled, again.

"I want the big black dog!"

"I want the little black dog!"

"I want Mickey!"

There was no slowing them down until the dogs were leashed up, and the leashes were in the correct hands.

Big Black Dog, Little Black Dog, and Mickey

Up they went to the picnic area under strict instructions to keep the dogs away from Julie. Around and around they marched with the dogs in perfect formation except Holly, who looked like she was ricocheting around the yard at the end of her lead. Breanna was keeping up with her, despite the size nine boats covering her feet.

Somehow, Jenae ended up with Solo after a while. She was having trouble getting him to get up from a down position. She was tugging at him, but he wouldn't budge. Her slight frame couldn't hold a candle to his 95 pounds. I told her to say, "Solo … Come!" and just start walking. She did … he did … and off they marched.

Making Boxes

After they had as much fun as they could handle with the dogs, we secured the dogs in the pen, and went off to find something to do in the house. (Dog lovers might be upset about the dogs having to stay in the pen, but usually, on Saturday, they spent the day with Harry, padding after him wherever he went … to the TV room, to the Barn, to the Waterfall. However, this was a Tea Party day … Harry was GONE!)

I had printed some pretty box patterns on card stock, but they hadn't yet been cut out and folded. Stephanie, Brittany, and I helped the smaller girls select the patterns they wanted. We had a little discussion about what was on the sheet so they could try to visualize what the finished product might look like. Kimberly was up for independent work. Stephanie helped Breanna, while Brittany helped Jenae. Connie was there for anyone who needed a little extra one-on-one. Everyone was totally absorbed in the little boxes for the longest time. Meanwhile, Carol and Janet visited out in the back yard watching Julie … It brought back memories of the time Connie and I had left Carol to fend for herself with a bunch of little girls playing "golf-croquet." Carol's revenge was sweet.

Time for Tea

After a little cutting, folding, and pasting, the girls were positively thrilled with their boxes. It was finally time for tea. Yellow jackets dictated the tea would be served indoors. Quickly, all the scraps of paper were swept up and tossed. The little girls sat patiently at the table on instructions not to eat anything until everyone was served. Cookies, tarts, and tea were quickly assembled, and the girls, young and old, were invited to participate. That year, the sugar bowl was monitored more closely than in past years ... consequently, nothing exciting happened. I was surprised there were even a couple of cookies left after the little girls finished their tea.

Pictures on the Sofa

By that time, everyone was tired. It was well after 4:30 p.m. That was a long time for adults to be in attendance, let alone children ... but ... all the boxes! We needed to have a picture of the whole group and all the boxes they had made. The tripod was already in place. All we had to do was assemble in front of, on, and in back of the sofa to get a group shot. Jenae, the five-year-old, who had been extremely patient, was starting to lose it and was refusing to get in the picture. Finally, she acquiesced. After several tries, I got some good shots. Every shot was to have been the last one. When I was finished, I happened to look at the last one, only to find I had cut Stephanie and Brittany out of the picture. We had to do it yet another time. After two more shots, Jenae had had it. She burst into tears, wailing, "I'm tired of the Tea Party!" The Tea Party ended abruptly! Within ten minutes, everyone was out the door. Hugs, boxes,

thank-yous, leftovers … everyone and everything … GONE!
… pretty funny!

Not the Last Picture Snapped

The Tenth Annual Ladies' Tea Party

August 28, 2005

The night before the Tenth Annual Ladies' Tea Party was dedicated to completing the grocery shopping, to making the chicken salad, to setting out tables chairs and cutlery, and to the next day's baking. Bright and early on the morning of the Tea Party, while I was still waking up, I made an Apple Crisp. The smell got the day started right. The rest of the morning was a normal Sunday morning. The church service lasted a little longer than usual, and I didn't get home until about 1:00 p.m. I was glad we had set the start time at 2:00 p.m.

I had lots of time to get things set up for the table, to put individual scoops of chicken salad on lettuce leaves, to make the sandwiches (cucumber/olive as well as almond-butter/banana), and to get myself settled. Everything was ready to go at 2:00 p.m., except ... as I discovered later ... the batteries in the camera.

The Entourage

Carol came with Brittany and a fabulous fruit salad. Connie followed soon after with a bacon-topped layered salad. We had a nice little chat waiting for Janet to come with a carful of little ladies:

Brittany was almost fifteen. She already had her class schedule for her first year at Skyview High School, and was anxious to get her learner's permit.

Jenae was six and very much at home wherever she went. She marched in with some fancy miniature Raspberry Muffinettes, and an assortment of herb teas in a pretty pink bag. Julie, Jenae's younger sister, was four and was able to come this year.

Kiersten was eight. It was her second year. She was very good with dogs. Valerie, her sister, was twelve. She was going into her second year at Alki Middle School. She and Kiersten brought some fragrant carnations and other flowers, which looked great in my large cut glass vase. Everybody snapped a picture of the two girls peeking out from behind the flowers.

Boris is a Star

I had wondered what we'd do first, but Boris stole the show. Most of the little ladies wanted a turn at feeding him a grape. Boris had always been temperamental. He quickly moved over to the nasty side of the scale when he when he had more than one grape poked at him! Not to be deterred, they all wanted to pet him. I don't know why everyone gravitates to the biter. It's a dangerous situation for whoever holds him … that would be me. Hoping for the best, I took Boris from the cage, and finally managed to cover his head and coo to him while all the girls took turns petting his back and wing feathers. I was surprised at how good he was during all this petting, but of course none of us had had any sugar yet!

On Jenae's suggestion, Boris got to come into the house for the Tea Party. He liked it. In fact, he really enjoyed the attention.

Whenever there was a lull in the activities, the girls went over to fuss with Boris. I was glad I had gotten him out for a petting opportunity ... and glad they didn't try to do it on their own!

Sneaking Around

We had a little juice to start, and then looked for the dogs so they could join us as we went down to feed the fish. The dogs were nowhere to be found! The girls looked in the pen; I looked in the basement ... nothing. Finally, I went over to the barn and discovered Harry had locked himself in with the dogs and was not about to unlock the door. He's no fool! I didn't have a key handy, so I had to go around to the other door. I told the girls to wait out front, but at least two sets of eyes watched me go through the potting area to the far side. Not wanting them to discover the second entry, I told them to go back to the first door, while I stole through the barn, passing Harry, who was working on his stained-glass project. I promised him no one would invade his territory. I ducked down to avoid the windows, unlocked the door, and retraced my steps as fast as I could. Once back with the girls, I opened the door a crack and let one dog out ... Holly. Jenae put her on a six-foot leash. I opened it a crack again and out came Solo. Kiersten put him on a short leash. Once more, just a crack, and Mickey came out to be walked by Valerie. Off we went to the pond. Each was happy with the dog she had. What an easy year. (It's a good thing Tessie, Marg's wild French Brittany Spaniel, wasn't visiting for the day!)

The Barn Door Opened Just a Crack

When we got to the Upper Pond, Jenae showed Kiersten and
Valerie how to throw a scoopful of food to the fish. They all
took turns. There was plenty of food, and there were plenty of
opportunities. In fact, their desire to toss food dissipated one
scoopful before the bucket was empty. Everything seemed to
be going smoothly. This was not a bad omen because the whole
day went smoothly ... except, on the way down to the pond, my

camera told me the "freshly charged" batteries I had inserted earlier needed to be recharged!

A Hidden Location

After Valerie got a chance to see the trout, we went back to the house to start our luncheon. Valerie wanted to know where we were going to eat. I told her it was a hidden spot … somewhere between the Forest and the Maid's Garden. It's a shady little area hidden behind an herbaceous island in the backyard lawn. There is plenty of room for a picnic table between the island and the bushes on the property line. Very secluded, flat, and shaded … which we all appreciated.

Before we went out, Kiersten honored us by saying a blessing for the food, and then by saying the Norwegian blessing she knew (with a little help from Valerie). And if that wasn't good enough, we all chimed in with the Blessing we've been familiar with since childhood: "Bless us, O Lord, and these Thy gifts, which we are about to receive, from Thy bounty, through Christ, our Lord. Amen."

Speed Buffet

The whole ritual of filling our plates went exceptionally well. It was the second time the sandwiches had been made in advance.

The first time was the first year. Having all the sandwiches pre-made helped the older ladies keep pace with the little ladies, who filled their plates first.

An Unexpected Treat

Jenae positioned herself at the door and held it open for people who were coming and going. I thought it was exceptionally considerate of her, especially since her plate was already out on the picnic table. Finally, we all found our way outside. Even Janet and Julie managed to come out before we had finished eating. (There's something magical about the size of a six-year-old's fingers and the holes in a black olive!)

Ropes and Bassinettes

It was no surprise Jenae and Kiersten finished first. After excusing themselves, they went to play with the rope still hanging off the deck ... they came back pretty soon when they discovered it's pretty easy to bump your shoulder on the post if you're not careful. They each got a turn sitting in the blue "bassinette" (aka hanging chair) and finally came back to see us again.

Pasties

Our next project was to design and assemble some bookmarks with glue sticks ... the kind that fold over the page, and snap together with magnets. We had dozens of old card-fronts to choose from for design, color, or just backgrounds. Brittany, Valerie, Jenae, Kiersten, and I worked hard on our projects for what must have been at least a half hour. Finally, it was time for tea.

Tea - The Untold Story

As we moved things to and fro, getting all set up, it was time to fill the creamer. The Half-and-Half was dated September 24, but the refrigerator had been running warmer than normal while the freezer had been running colder than normal. I knew it was important to give it the smell test. As I feared, the cream was a little worse for the wear and had a bumpy ride into the creamer. We tried to save the situation by substituting milk, but I was pretty sure we wouldn't find what we needed in the milk carton ... and I was right. The milk went for a bumpy ride down the drain with a caution to the little eyes and noses around the sink: "Look, but don't smell!" The girls were disappointed there wouldn't be any cream, but we solved that dilemma by putting a tiny scoop of vanilla ice cream on everyone's dessert plate. Dessert was a tart Apple Crisp, a highly sweetened Raspberry Muffin-ette, and a mini-scoop of Vanilla Ice Cream. The girls managed just fine at the table, but the older ladies were all having a little trouble sitting on the sofas balancing their tea and dessert.

Group Photo

Jenae and Kiersten wanted to go down to the pond again. I should have told them to go ahead. Foolish me. Instead, we watched them get wound up because of the sugar. It was good they stayed up at the house, though, because we got a nice group photo.

Ciao Bella

Janet called John as we were winding down and told him to bring Bella for a visit. Bella was their new ten-week-old Boxer puppy. While we were waiting for John, the wind picked up. It appeared the big storm, scheduled for Sunday evening, was about to hit. When John drove up, Harry came out of the barn to say hi, and almost immediately our three dogs ran out to meet Bella. Fortunately, they all seemed to get along great. Holly tried to let Bella know we have house rules, but Bella just accepted there were rules and went on with life. Mickey wasn't too sure about Bella, but everyone got along just fine … with Harry present!

Stormy Ending

After strapping Julie in the car seat, Janet and I were having one last chat. Before she could get in the car, Jenae jumped out and came around to tell her they'd better get going because the "storm is blowin' in!" And thus ended a decade of Annual Ladies' Tea Parties!

End of an Era

It's a shame Stephanie and Brittany and Jenae moved away. Otherwise, we would have kept on having our little tea parties. Much like enjoying Christmas mornings, you really have to appreciate what you have when you can because the little ones do grow up fast! Things change.

PART FOUR

STEPPING OUT

Prelude

Harry and I both had full-time jobs. Although re-creating and maintaining Two Ponds kept me busy, there was still plenty of time to step out and teach Sunday School. Who knew kids could be so adaptable?

Sunday School Super Bowl

2013

Every week, I prayed often during the week for the Holy Spirit's inspiration in preparation for our Sunday School class. This week was no exception. But nothing was coming to mind.

Finally, late Saturday night, I printed out the final chapters of Matthew, Mark, Luke, and John, and the first two chapters of Acts of the Apostles. I figured we'd look at Jesus's last words to His disciples and apply it to our lives. We'd been studying the minds of the Jews at the time of Christ for the last couple of weeks. I thought looking at the period from the Resurrection through Pentecost would be a natural follow-up. I went over and over the text, paring out about half of it so I only had the highlights … I didn't want to lose the kids' attention halfway through class. Usually, after doing that much work, I get at least some inspiration and can then develop a plan of how the class might proceed. But still I was coming up empty.

I called it a night, but continued to pray my favorite Sunday-School prayer from Psalm 51 and the associated hymn: "Create in me a pure heart, O God, and renew a right spirit within me. Cast me not away from Your presence, O Lord, take not your Holy Spirit from me; restore in me the joy of Your salvation, and renew a right spirit within me."

On the drive to church the next morning, I decided we'd have a mock football game. It was, after all, Super Bowl Sunday. I figured the game would have something to do with the six pages of text I'd printed about Jesus's last instructions. (As it turned out, I didn't use any of those pages at all.) As usual, the kids would have to answer questions and would get points somehow. (I found myself wishing I had a whistle with me.)

When I got to church and entered our room, I drew a table on the board:

Football Today	
San Francisco 49ers	Baltimore Ravens

Then I left for worship time in the sanctuary. About the time I sat down, I got an idea to make a football field. After that, I mentally let everything go and paid attention to worship time.

When worship was over, I went to class, pulled out a 33" by 33" piece of paper, folded it in half, made some tick marks, and had the kids help me draw the yard lines on this "football field." One of the kids rolled up a small piece of paper towel and twisted the ends so it had the faint resemblance to a football.

I chose two quarterbacks. Everyone who wanted to be a Raven sat on one side of the table (five of them). The other three wanted to be 49ers. I really wanted it to be balanced, so I whispered to the fifth Raven he should be a 49er because the 49ers were going to win. Nope. He wanted to be a Raven with all his buddies. It was complicated by the fact one of the boys was named Christian, but at least the two Jacobs were on different teams.

Absolutely no one had a coin, not even me. I took a blunt pair of scissors and had the quarterbacks call "heads" or "tails." I spun the scissors. The 49ers won the "spin" and elected to have the other team receive … a very smart move since none of us, including me, knew the rules of the game, yet.

Teamwork Under Stress

Christian was the Raven's quarterback. I told him he had to tell all about one of the things we've learned in the past quarter. He understood. He started talking about Jesus and the Second Coming. He mentioned the word "Rapture." I was standing behind Jacob, a 49er, leaning over him with my index finger on the football. It was as if everything disappeared but the football. It started at the 49ers' twenty-yard-line and advanced slowly to the thirty, the forty, and center field as Christian told what he'd learned. But then, Christian ran out of things to say and panicked as the football came to a standstill. We were all trying to make up a rule to help. His team jumped in and told him to throw a lateral pass. He passed to Eli. Eli restated some of Christian's story (the football retraced some of its progress). As Eli filled in more of the story, the football approached the

Raven's goal line. Eli "threw" a lateral pass to James, who completed the story.

"TOUCHDOWN! ... SIX POINTS!"

Conversions

We had to figure out how to get the extra point(s) after touchdown.

I told the Ravens to run over to the far corner of the room and figure out a seven-letter word I was thinking of. I wrote the word on the board but kept it hidden. Then, I told them they had to figure it out, but only the quarterback could tell me the answer. I gave them a clue: it was a word someone had already said.

I gave them some time and then raised two fingers to my mouth making a shrill whistle.

"THWEET!"

Everyone was surprised, but they recovered as Christian said "MESSIAH."

What a great word. I wished I'd thought of it. But the word I had written on the board was "RAPTURE." I gave them one point for a great seven-letter word and told them they would have had two points if they had guessed "RAPTURE." Everyone was satisfied with that rule.

Success with the Good Samaritan

Things were looking good. The Ravens had seven points. They punted to the 49ers, and the ball started on the Raven's twenty-yard line. Olivia, the quarterback, passed to David, who started to tell the story of the Good Samaritan (from our study on parables). David did a good job, but the Ravens were right on his case with every word he spoke. (Oh, those Ravens!) Under duress, he started to get confused and lateralled to Olivia, who finished the story.

"TOUCHDOWN! ... SIX POINTS!"

Olivia and her two teammates went to the opposite corner of the room (near the door) and conferred to see if they could get their extra point. My seven-letter word was "PARABLE," but they didn't get it. However, they had an equally good word, and it had the right number of letters.

"ONE POINT! THE SCORE IS TIED ... Seven-all!"

Bored and Competitive

These kids were only ten years old. A couple of the Ravens (Christian and Eli) had gotten antsy and left the table while I was recording the 49ers' point after touchdown. It was the Ravens' ball on the 49ers' twenty-yard line. The Ravens got a penalty because not all the players were at their table. Christian came back, but Eli was still holed up under the chairs against the wall (probably playing fort). They got another five-yard penalty. I said if the football backed into the end zone it would be a "touchback." I'm not sure if that was a proper application of "touchback," but James and Jacob are fierce competitors, and neither wanted anything that looked like a penalty. They ran over, grabbed Eli by the arms, and dragged him back to the table!

Someone suggested we toss a roll of painter's tape to the person who should be speaking so we'd know who "had the ball." Good idea! Christian tossed the tape to James. James told the story of the Sermon on the Mount (from the Miracle Lesson of our Gospel series). There was some question about the number of loaves and fishes, so they made a few lateral transfers until the team zeroed in on the correct facts. Then, we made another rule: if the facts weren't right, the other team could intercept the ball (fortunately we never had to switch teams in the middle of one team's rush to the goal line). The story finally got finished.

"TOUCHDOWN! … SIX MORE POINTS!"

They all ran for the corner.

I said I needed a six-letter word, but they could give me a five-letter word or both. They collaborated.

"THWEET!"

Christian guessed "BREAD."

"Great try! But the two-point words were 'SERMON' or 'MOUNT'." They all groaned.

"ONE POINT!"

Grace and Kindness

Tall Jacob was on the 49er's team. He has always been a little shy so I was never sure how much he really knew. I quietly asked him, "Do you know a Bible story?"

"Uh-huh."

"What about?"

"John the Baptist."

"Okay." We were ready. Olivia passed the football to Jacob. He started telling the story. He was really into the spirit of the game. Words were pouring out of his mouth faster than I've ever heard from him, but I couldn't understand any of them. The football was moving fast down the field. I kept listening, but for the life of me, I couldn't figure out what story he was telling. The football was getting down to the 49ers' twenty-yard line. In another twenty yards, I was expected to announce a touchdown. I was starting to panic. Jacob was still talking a blue streak. I looked pleadingly at Olivia, who shrugged and mouthed "Noah's Ark?" Then she leaned in to Jacob with grace and kindness and asked, "Is it Noah's Ark?"

"Uh-huh."

The scrunched and twisted paper-towel football kept moving closer to the end zone. We were at the goal line. "Are you finished?" I asked.

"Uh-huh."

"TOUCHDOWN! … SIX POINTS!"

Jacob got up and headed for the door … just like he did every week. I thought he was going home. I looked at the door. His mom hadn't come yet. "Don't leave yet, Sweetheart, we're still playing the game." Then I realized he was just trying to go to the corner to get a point after touchdown. He really was into it! I told them I needed a three-letter word. They conferred.

"THWEET!"

Olivia announced, "ARK."

"YES!" We had ourselves a game!

Cross or Thief

Blond Jacob and Jed, two of the Ravens, were stoked. Jacob knows tons of facts and did a great job when it was his turn. Jed, on the other hand, can be a little shy when put on the spot. I was worried, but he caught the ball and started relating the story about the two thieves who were hung with Jesus. Half-way through, he lateralled to James, who finished the story with a so-called fact that startled everyone, including me. It was amazing how they all said, "What?" at the same time. (In that moment, I realized these kids are truly thinking for themselves and not just parroting what people, including me, are telling them.) Since the startling revelation was off topic, we set it aside until later. The decibel level was climbing. "THIEF" was the word I wrote on the board. I thought maybe I should use "CROSS," but decided to stick with "THIEF." The Ravens all started talking at once: "Cross ... no ... Thief ... no ... Cross, Cross, CROSS!" they screamed. It looked like James and Jacob were going to steamroll right over Christian. (I wished I'd written "CROSS" on the board.)

"THWEET!"

"Christian, what's your answer?"

Christian wasn't intimidated. He shouted, "THIEF!"

I moved aside revealing "THIEF."

"RIGHT! ... TWO POINTS!"

The Ravens were jumping and screaming out of their minds!

One or Two Facts

Olivia did a little ditty the kids knew from their weekday schooling ... it was fifty words that take you through the whole Bible. She got some of the words wrong, and the Ravens verbally pounced on her. She fumbled. They hollered, thinking they had the ball, but I asked her to explain what she'd said.

"Is it factual?"

"Yes."

I gave the ruling: "She recovered the ball and defended her position so she gets to continue! ... SECOND DOWN." I had her turn around, plug her ears, and say her ditty again. She whipped right through it.

"SEVEN MORE POINTS!"

A Thirteen-Letter Word

David gave us a beautiful concise rendition of the suffering, death, and resurrection of Jesus, complete with the attitude of many of the Pharisees ... for another touchdown. As the 49ers gathered in the corner, I asked them for a twelve-letter word. I knew it would be tough but hoped they'd get "RESURRECTION." Then I had a brain cramp and couldn't remember if it had one or two s's. I quietly asked James, the Raven, who started spelling "R-E-S-S-U." I told the 49ers they needed to find a thirteen-letter word. I had hoped they heard James spelling the beginning of the word, but they didn't. However, they did come up with a great three-syllable word: "HYPOCRITE."

I told them the word was "RESURRECTION," but started counting the letters in "HYPOCRITE," and I'll be darned if there weren't thirteen letters. (The 49ers were behind and needed the point.)

"ONE MORE POINT!"

James, always the stickler, squealed, "Mrs. Hoffman, there aren't thirteen letters in 'HYPOCRITE'!"

"Yes, there are," I countered. I ticked them off on my fingers as I spelled aloud "H-Y-P-O-C-R-I-T-E." My fingers were flying faster than my spelling. I didn't want to take any team's points away, so each time I counted the letters in that nine-letter word, my fingers declared thirteen. Pretty soon, James realized no matter how many times I counted, "HYPOCRITE" would always be a thirteen-letter word, so the 49ers got their point. I still can't believe he let me get away with that!

Hoarse

We were at the last play of the game. The 49ers told a nice story about how the angel appeared to Mary and announced she was going to have a baby even though she wasn't married. Then the angel appeared to her cousin, and told her she was going to have a son, too. (The timing was a little off, but it was late in the class. I felt I could let a few errors go unchallenged.)

After their touchdown, the 49ers conflabbed in the corner. They needed two points to tie.

The Ravens were going crazy, beating their palms on the table and stomping their feet … the noise level was peaking. I transformed into being a stadium announcer, shouting: "LADIES

AND GENTLEMEN, THIS CROWD IS GOING WILD!"
They made even more noise.

The 49ers fussed and fussed. They had to come up with a six-letter word to tie the game. In the meantime, I had written the word "VIRGIN" on the board and was hiding it. Finally, Olivia announced, "MANGER!" It was a good try, but I stepped aside exposing the word "VIRGIN!"

The Ravens screamed!

I screeched at the top of my lungs: "THE BALTIMORE RAVENS HAVE WON THE SUPERBOWL!"

Best Sunday School Class ever!

Kudos

I know for a fact, none of this could have been possible without prayer. Here's one of my favorite verses to prove it:

Trust in the Lord with all your heart,

and lean not on your own understanding;

In everything you do, put God first,

and He shall direct your paths.

-- Proverbs 3:5-6

Afterthought

There are two walls of normal construction separating the Sunday School room from the sanctuary. I had gotten so caught up in the moment I didn't stop to think about whether or not we could be heard. Well, no one ever said anything, so it must not have been a problem.

The First Three Christians

One week, in Sunday School, we were concentrating on a review of the New Testament. I wanted to solidify the lessons we had learned over the past few months. Mr. Moeller, the Children's Ministry leader, was joining us for our finale.

The kids were expecting prizes. All year long, I had been struggling with what to do for prizes. Finally, I decided homemade cookies would be the best. I had tried bringing homemade candy one day, but three of the kids turned it down. Knowing food isn't a motivator for these kids, I crocheted Oreo cookies. They looked real. They would last a lot longer than the real thing.

The plan was elaborate, but it had to look simple. It had been a lot of work coming up with questions (Multiple Choice, True or False, and FillIn) for the Old Testament review. During the New Testament study, I had the kids make up questions (with answers) for our final review. That helped me know if they were getting it and it made it easier for them to get the answers during the test. When all was said and done, I had about 60 questions and answers.

I went to The Party Zone and got a package of water balloons (they hold up better than the regular ones). As luck would have it, there were 60 in a pack! On Friday, I blew up the colorful balloons and tied a shiny sparkling fifteen-inch ribbon to each. Each was about the size of a soda can. Each was numbered.

I rearranged the questions, numbering them so at least one of the digits for each of the hardest questions was a "one" (1, 10, 11, 12, 13, …, 41, 51). You get the picture? I divided the class. Kids on the left, Mr. Moeller on the right. There was only one rule: Answer correctly and your team could keep the balloons!

When the kids started coming in, I singled out the one I knew was dreading the "test." I asked him if he'd like to be the Balloon Guy. I told him it would be his job to choose a numbered balloon for each question and give it to the side whose turn it was, but warned him he wouldn't be able to participate in the test questions and asked if it was okay with him. He said it was good! Then I tried to get him to understand the concept of giving Mr. Moeller a balloon with a one in the number … I could tell it wasn't clicking … too bad. I figured I'd have to keep an eye on him. (It's hard for me to understand how different people are. This little guy didn't get numbers … I'm a mathematician … I don't know how to not get numbers … but I knew enough to be sensitive to him!) I told him I was going to ask for a volunteer, and he'd better stick his hand up right away. He was primed.

After we prayed, I handed out Certificates of Completion. They had really learned a lot during the year. Then we dug into the game. I asked for a volunteer to help me hand out balloons. Up went Balloon Guy's hand … he was immediately chosen. Rock/

Paper/Scissors gave us a Team Captain for the kids and helped us figure out who went first: Mr. Moeller was up first. Balloon Guy gave him a balloon … "23." I had to retract it … no "one" in the number. I gave Balloon Guy the "31" balloon which he passed to Mr. Moeller. Thankfully, Mr. Moeller didn't insist on having question "23." We were back on track with question "31." This first question was a dilly … you had to have been in the class to understand the answer. He guessed his way into the correct answer and I had the kids show him why he got it right. We were off and running. Easy questions to the kids, hard questions to Mr. Moeller. But one very special question was set aside for the end!

Balloon Guy was having a lot of trouble selecting balloons with a one in the number. I had to help quite a lot and hoped the rigging of the questions wasn't too noticeable. Mr. Moeller missed a question. All his balloons went over to the other side! Back and forth we went. Finally, the kids missed a question. All their balloons went over to Mr. Moeller! After one-half hour, the kids were getting restless. We were about two-thirds of the way through the game. By this time, Balloon Guy was more interested in making static electricity to get the balloons to stick to his head. One of the kids abandoned his team and went to help Mr. Moeller. The kids were moving everywhere and the noise level was rising. Mr. Moeller had about eighty percent of the balloons. We were nearing the end. At that point, there were about three kids surrounding Balloon Guy, all working furiously to get balloons to stick to his head. Mr. Moeller got a tough question. It looked like he was going to miss it and would lose all his balloons (Ooh, I didn't want that to happen too soon.) The kids struggled with it, too. It was just too hard.

Finally, Mr. Moeller got a tiny part of it, so I gave him the benefit of the doubt. The kids didn't think it was fair but forgot about fairness as we proceeded to the next question.

Finally, there was only one more balloon left and as "fortune" would have it, it was Mr. Moeller's turn. He had most of the balloons. It looked like he was going to win the game. But this was a very special question … a ringer. I laid it out there, "Name the first three Christians!" Mr. Moeller was stumped. The kids were really excited, jumping all around. They knew the answer … at least they remembered part of it … and Mr. Moeller was struggling. This was for all the balloons! The kids could taste victory!

We know a Christian is one who believes Jesus Christ is God. Mr. Moeller got the first … it was Mary, who was informed by an angel (Luke 1:35-38). The second was intuitive: There's no way Mary didn't tell Joseph everything the Angel said, and we know he believed her and trusted God. So Joseph was the second Christian. The third? … Mr. Moeller was scratching his head … I had to give him the answer: John the Baptist. Mary went to see her cousin, Elizabeth. As she approached the house, she called out. Even before Elizabeth saw Mary … "At the sound of Mary's greeting, Elizabeth's child leaped within her" (Luke 1:41).

With that, everyone grabbed their certificates, homemade cookies, and all the balloons they wanted. Off they went whooping and hollering down the whole length of the hall!

Cousin Cathy and I stayed behind laughing and tidying up … it always amazes me how good God is to these kids … and to us.

Are You a Jew?

One day, we were reviewing the Old Testament lessons and getting ready to study the New Testament. In the process, I had the kids tell me what they knew about several famous men in the Bible and how they fit into the big picture. The last one was Paul, whose claim to fame was taking the Gospel to the Gentiles. I needed to make sure the kids knew they should appreciate what Paul did for them, so I asked, "Who's a Gentile?"

I pointed to one of my Hispanic boys and asked, "Are you a Jew or a Gentile?"

Well, I guess it wasn't such a simple question because he said he was a Jew.

Then, the other Hispanic boy in the class said he was a Jew, as did the little Italian boy. His buddy, the Irish kid, was leaning forward telling me he was a Jew before I could get them reined in. I'll bet if I had a show of hands, 75 percent of them would have said they were Jews. I corrected the situation as best I could without laughing.

Who knew it was important to define words before using them!

Re-Counting VBS

Vacation Bible School, VBS, is a one-week program designed around nationwide preplanned themes, to teach children of all ages about Jesus. People come from all parts of the community, not just the congregation of the hosting church. The safety of the children is paramount! In 2019, the theme we chose was "To Mars and Beyond." It was a galactic experience of learning and growing with God through music, crafts, science, food, and lots of fun! When I volunteered to be an assistant, I had no idea how exasperating it would be to keep track of little people. The donations given during the week benefitted Lutheran Community Services. The Vancouver Office focuses on immigrant and refugee resettlement. Unable to explain what that meant in basic words, I told the children the donations went to help sick children. Every VBS is centered around a Bible verse. The Bible verse that went with "To Mars and Beyond" was from Ephesians 3:20: "Glory to God Who is able to do far beyond all that we could ask or imagine by God's power at work within us." The following is a daily summary of the events and struggles in one of the pre-school classes.

Day: Monday

Lesson: Go beyond with Faith

Bible Story: Daniel in the Lion's Den

The Tall Assistant looked at her clipboard. It was the first day of Vacation Bible School. She had never been surrounded by so many four- and five-year-olds. There were 45 in all, but as she counted the names on her clipboard, she realized there were only twelve in her class. She counted by two's: 2 - 4 - 6 - 8 - 10 - 12 - 13! Uh-Oh! She counted the parents' signatures: 2 - 4 - 6 - 8 - 10 - 12. Twelve children had signed in. She counted the children again: 2 - 4 - 6 - 8 - 10 - 12 - 13! Thirteen children were present. She was horrified. Had she failed to get a signature with an incoming child? She started matching the children to the signatures. They were all new to her. She was forced to read the name tags on the front of each t-shirt. One by one she checked them off: Molly, Jannie, Carlton, Gennie, Minnie, Molly … wait, she had already checked Molly. The children were moving randomly all around the classroom! She had to start over. Eventually, with the help of the Kindly Leader, she discovered the extra child was Gerald. He was not on her list. She wondered where in the world he had come from. Frantically, she ran to the next room. "Do you have a Gerald?"

"Yes, but he's not here!" responded the Room Assistant, quickly and apprehensively.

"Oh good, we've got him. Let's let him stay in our classroom until it's time to go home." The Assistants had come to an agreement. (It turned out there was an adjoining bathroom between the two rooms, unbeknownst to the leaders, but definitely beknownst to Gerald.)

The day continued peacefully enough. The Tall Assistant did whatever the Kindly Leader beckoned. The Youthful Helper worked well with the children. The Three formed a good team.

"US against THEM ..." the notion drifted through each of their minds ... "and US is winning."

The Kindly Leader told the Bible story. Line up, process to Sanctuary, return ... oh my goodness, where did all the snacks come from? "Wash your hands before snacks," reminded the Kindly Leader. Crafts, outside play time, Bible story recap, then dismissal. During the Bible story recap, the Tall Assistant repeated the story using slightly different words. It was time to take donations, but only one child had brought money for a donation. The Tall Assistant scratched her head and mused, "This will not do."

Day: Tuesday

Lesson: Go beyond with Boldness

Bible Story: Queen Esther

Note: Gerald tried to get back into our class three times but we were wise to him.

The Tall Assistant grabbed the clipboard and counted the children: 2 - 4 - 6 - 8 - 10 - 11. Then she counted the parents' signatures: 2 - 4 - 6 - 8 - 10 - 12. Oh no, this time she was missing a child. She peered over the bookcase on the right ... not there. She peered over the bookcase on the left ... not there. She recounted: 2 - 4 - 6 - 8 - 10 - 11. Still not good enough. She frantically enlisted the aid of the Youthful Helper. He counted out loud: "2 - 4 - 6 - 8 - 10 - 11." They were both breaking out in a sweat. "Oh wait," he said in the softest of voices, "there's another one in the back corner." Finally, all was as it should be.

The retelling of the Bible story got much more interesting when the Tall Assistant revealed a Ziploc bag full of pennies. Students who remembered portions of the Bible story were rewarded with a penny or two. One little Socialist repeatedly asked for a penny without first answering a question (he must have been a four-year-old). After a good number of pennies had been distributed, the Tall Assistant told the children they had earned their money and could keep it if they wished … however … if they wanted to donate it to help sick people, they could put some or all of their pennies in the donation cup. "I'll keep my eyes closed," she promised, as she held out the cup. Pennies clattered into the cup like popcorn popping. As the clatter slowed, she opened her eyes, slightly. "Your eyes are open!" someone cried. Immediately, she closed them. Finally, it was quiet. She opened her eyes and looked up at the Kindly Leader … they both grinned. (The Kindly Leader later told her the faces were full of grimaces as many children struggled with the concept of giving.) Goodbyes were said, children were logged out, another day was complete.

Day: Wednesday

Lesson: Go beyond with Kindness

Bible Story: The Good Samaritan

This day proceeded with no snags. It was a very pleasant, normal day. During the recap of the Bible story, the Tall Assistant passed out another handful of pennies and invited the children once again to donate their booty to the cause for sick people.

She closed her eyes, passed the cup, and was a little surprised to hear only a little dribble of pennies hitting the bottom of the cup.

"Well, that was interesting," she thought. "They're getting wise to us."

Day: Thursday

Lesson: Go beyond with Thankfulness

Bible Story: Jesus Heals The Lepers

Note: US against THEM: US was still winning … only because THEM didn't realize the power they wielded.

When the time for retelling the Bible story came, the Tall Assistant passed out pennies as usual. Looking at the penny bag she realized there were way too many pennies remaining. She invited the children to say their special Bible verse: anyone who could say the verse … "Glory to God Who is able to do far beyond all that we could ask or imagine by God's power at work within us. - Ephesians 3:20" … would get five pennies. The excitement was unbelievable. After about 3 responses, the children were jumping up and down screaming "Glory to God … Glory to God!" Amazingly everyone … including the Socialist … earned at least five pennies. Once again, the Tall Assistant closed her eyes and passed the donation cup. She anticipated a barrage of pennies. But she could almost count them, individually, as she heard only about five pennies being dropped into the cup.

"Well," she thought, "that backfired!"

Day: Friday

Lesson: Go beyond with Hope

Bible Story: The Walk to Emmaus

Note: One of the girls had gone camping. As a result, there were only eleven children participating.

The children were beside themselves with happiness. They were enjoying Vacation Bible School. They knew they were coming to the last minutes, but there was no sadness. They were fully present in the moment. With the retelling of the Bible story, the Tall Assistant passed out a handful of pennies, and then stood up to her full height. She asked the children questions about the whole week. The remaining pennies tumbled from the heavens. The children were so excited they could hardly hold it in. The Tall Assistant took out the donation cup. She told the children, "There's a verse in the Bible which declares 'God loves a Cheerful Giver!'"

"Now you say it," she challenged.

"God loves a cheerful giver," came a few responses.

"Say it again!" she said with some urgency.

"God Loves a Cheerful Giver," they rang out in unison.

"ONE MORE TIME!"

"GOD LOVES A CHEERFUL GIVER!" they all screamed.

The Tall Assistant invited them to keep their money or donate it for sick people. She closed her eyes and held out the cup. Pennies flooded in from all directions. They had paid attention.

The cup got heavier and heavier. The children were truly Cheerful Givers. The Youthful Helper dipped into his pocket and pulled out a bill. Into the cup it went. The Kindly Leader scurried over to her purse and came back with another bill. The Tall Assistant realized it was time for her to pony-up. She put in yet another bill. The cup was passed around so the children could feel how heavy it was. They were so excited to be giving their money to help sick people … cheerfully.

Afterward, everyone went over to the Sanctuary. Two boys from the class were selected to take the donation cup up and pour the contents into the large communal fish bowl. Soon they were back in their seats. Out of habit, the Tall Assistant counted: 2 - 4 - 6 - 8 - 10. "Oh-no, not again!" she shuddered. She re-counted: 2 - 4 - 6 - 8 - 10! The Tall Assistant looked anxiously to the Kindly Leader. "Up there," the Kindly Leader indicated silently. The Tall Assistant saw the tiniest of the children standing up by the fish bowl, her body contorted as she was attempting to get the last of the pennies out of her left hip pocket … with her right hand. It would be the last donation deposited in the fish bowl.

A final march across the parking lot, some final snacks, a final craft, a final play period. Decorations came down, hugs were given, eleven children were checked out to eleven parents, blinds were closed. Relief!

It was a very satisfying week.

Epilogue

Oh … the stories I could tell. And tell them, I shall.

About the Author

Kathy Hoffman was born and raised in Portland, Oregon, with her six brothers. She has a BS in Mathematics and enjoyed a 28-year career as an engineer with the Bonneville Power Administration. She later volunteered as a math tutor, and then went on to sell and service insurance policies with her husband in his Vancouver, Washington, State Farm Agency … but her passion is, and has always been, laughter.

Watch for more humorous stories of life at Two Ponds when cold-hard reality slaps Hoffman in the face: "Christmas at Two Ponds: The Back Story," the second of the Two Ponds series, is expected to be published in 2022.